A red Sea, a Burning Bush and a plague of frogs

WRITTEN BY **Malc' Halliday**

CARTOONS BY **Ian Potter**

Scripture Union

© Malc' Halliday 2000
First published 2000

ISBN 1 85999 365 6

All rights reserved. No part of this publication may be reproduced, stored in a retrieval system, or transmitted, in any form or by any means, electronic, mechanical, photocopying, recording or otherwise, without the prior permission of Scripture Union.

The right of Malc' Halliday to be identified as author of this work has been asserted by him in accordance with the Copyright, Designs and Patents Act 1988.

The right of Ian Potter to be identified as illustrator of this work has been asserted by him in accordance with the Copyright, Designs and Patents Act 1988.

Scriptures quoted from the *Good News Bible* published by The Bible Societies/Harper Collins Publishers Ltd., UK, © American Bible Society, 1966, 1971, 1976, 1992.

British Library Cataloguing-in-Publication Data.
A catalogue record for this book is available from the British Library.

Printed and bound in Great Britain by Creative Print and Design (Wales), Ebbw Vale.

WHAT'S WHERE

Where's where?		3
Your guides		4
Introduction		5
1	Moses: the early years	7
2	Moses does a runner	17
3	Mission impossible	29
4	Free at last	39
5	Moaning, manna and miracles	50
6	Ten to one	58
7	The golden calf	69
8	God's house	76
9	Census and sensibility	86
10	On the brink	94
11	Wonky donkey	107
12	Moses: the final chapter	117

YOUR GUIDES

SHIMEI THE SMELLI

Alright! I'm Shimei. How are ya? I'd just like to say, 'Nice one for buying this book!' I'll be guiding you through the ins and outs, the ups and downs, the highs and lows, the tops and bottoms... not that there are many bottoms in here. You get the idea. Anyway, I'll be showing you around the book, and to help me with this enormous task is Benji.

BENJI THE BOOKWORM

Hi! I'm Benji – I've managed to worm my way (geddit?) into this book because Shimei is hopeless with numbers. He also smells awful, but that's another story. When you see me holding up a sign, if you like you can get your Bible out and read the 'official' version of the story.

SIBTHORPE THE LEGAL QUAIL

Greetings and salutations, esteemed readers! My name is Sibthorpe, and I am your Legal Quail – the editors couldn't afford a 'Legal Eagle' so they hired me, as I'm a lot cheaper. I shall be introducing you to some of the laws after the Ten Commandments, known in the trade as 'COOL RULES'.

INTRODUCTION

This is a rags to riches to rags story. It is the tale of someone who as a boy, floated *on* water and, as a man, walked *through* water, and despite many trials and tribulations, never allowed water (or anything else for that matter) to overwhelm him.

Our story takes us on a journey. From slave villages to palaces, across deserts and into the hills. Through cities and the waters of a mighty sea. A journey where God did the map-reading and people learned to follow. If that's the sort of journey you're up for, then pack your sarnies (unleavened bread only please), gird up your loins (whatever that means) and let's go.

We begin in the palace of a king. It is late at night, and through the palace corridors comes the sound of a court at peace with itself and the murmurs of snoring in a variety of pitches and tones. However, in one room, someone was still awake. Push the door gently and let's go in...

1 MOSES: THE EARLY YEARS

EXODUS 1:1-22

Pharoah, the King of Egypt, couldn't sleep. He was ruler of this great nation, worshipped as a god and he couldn't sleep. It was the babies that did it. Every time he closed his eyes: Hebrew babies – hundreds, thousands, millions, billions... and whatever comes after that. He tried counting them: / // /// //// ///// existing ////// /////// //////// ///////// n (of course he counted in hieroglyphs), but the more he counted the more babies appeared.

Pharaoh, as he was called, just like his father, and his father before him (distinct lack of imagination in the Egyptian royal family), got up and looked out from his bedroom over the two great cities being built: Pithom and Raamses. Cities that would be used to store food. It was 400 years since that Hebrew Joseph had saved the nation from famine and starvation, and this Pharaoh wanted to be certain that it didn't happen again. Four hundred years ago it had

seemed the decent thing to allow Joseph, his dad Jacob and his family to come and live in Egypt. But the family grew (and grew and grew) until now there were thousands of Jacob's descendants filling up the place.

Quite frankly, Pharaoh (the same one who couldn't sleep, not to be confused with his father [Pharaoh] and his grandfather [Pharaoh] or his son who would one day be... you guessed it...), anyway *this* Pharaoh panicked. Suppose the Hebrews wanted to take over? Suppose they joined up with the Egyptians' enemies and conquered the land? Suppose...? And once he'd started supposing he couldn't stop. Something had to be done.

His first idea was to make the Hebrews his slaves. If he put them to work, building the great store-cities he was looking at now, then at the end of the day they'd be too worn out to think about subterfuge, double-dealing and other dastardly deeds. And they would certainly have no energy for producing millions more babies.

It didn't work. The cities were being built, and the slaves were tired, but it seems you can no more stop the world from making babies than you can stop your teacher from dishing out homework, or Carol Vorderman making TV programmes. The babies kept coming, the people were getting stronger and Pharaoh still couldn't sleep.

His second-best brilliant idea was to have a word with the midwives: the women who were always there when the Hebrew women were giving birth. Shiphrah and Puah (I am *not* making these names up) were invited by Pharaoh to explore a new method of population control. It was simple really. If the newborn baby was a boy[1] they delivered a swift blow to the head instead of a light slap to the behind.

---

[1] I know, you're asking yourself how they could tell. Dear innocent reader, there is an easy method – boys have dirty fingernails – simple.

Unfortunately, Shippy and Puey (to their friends) didn't see it that way. They thought their job was to help life *start*, not bring it to a sudden end. So they didn't do it. They told Pharaoh that no sooner had they turned their backs to boil the water (an essential feature of all births throughout history) than the little things arrived and... well, what could *they* do?

The babies kept on coming, the people were getting stronger and Pharaoh couldn't sleep.

Now, as he looked out across his kingdom, and as the sun rose, he thought of a plan so horrible that those of you of a nervous disposition should only continue reading in a dark room with your eyes shut.

EXODUS 2:1-10

Miriam couldn't sleep. It was her baby brother that did it. He was cute, adorable, cuddly and all those other gooey things, but he was also a boy and Pharaoh didn't want him around. At his first cry or whimper, Miriam had to rush to quieten him. Pharaoh's horrible plan had been to bypass the midwives and order his soldiers to patrol the Hebrew settlements. Any baby boys found gurgling, yelling or simply sucking their thumbs were thrown into the River Nile... and they weren't expected to find their way out. If the soldiers were seen approaching their village she would rush to hide him and do all she could to keep him quiet: fingers in his mouth, Horlicks in his bottle – in fact any of the tried and trusted family methods used throughout the centuries. For three months it had worked, but how long could they keep it up? He would start to crawl – probably right into the path of the soldiers. He would begin teething and, in a land where Calpol had yet to be invented, this meant screaming and lots of it. It was

surely only a matter of time... Miriam and her mother Jochabed made a decision. Strangely enough, the baby's father and older brother Aaron were not consulted. After all, Jochabed knew very well that the best man for a job is a woman, and so she just got on with things. The baby's father doesn't have much to do with this story at all in fact, but tuck Aaron's name away inside your memory banks – it could be useful. Anyway back to the action...

If the baby stayed, sooner or later he would be thrown into the River Nile. Strangely, the decision Jochabed made was to throw him into the Nile herself. Maybe he would die, but then again maybe the God she worshipped, the God of Jacob and Joseph, would protect her baby. God had promised Jacob centuries ago that his descendants would become great, and that one day God would take them to their own land. Why should her new-born son not be allowed to be part of that day when it came?

She set to work to

make a little boat for her boy. You can make one too. Here's how:
YOU WILL NEED:
PAPYRUS REEDS
(These grow over five metres high so be sure to ask for help when you cut them down)
TAR
BABY
STICKY-BACKED PLASTIC
WASHING UP BOTTLE[2]

1. Weave papyrus leaves into a basket shape
2. Put tar outside (to stop the water getting in) and inside (to stop the baby getting out)
3. Put baby in boat

Easy!!

WARNING
If the boat sinks and the baby drowns either:
a) start again but use more tar this time
   or
b) sell the idea to Pharaoh

Jochabed put the basket containing Moses into the river and

---

[2] The last two items are optional. Stick them in a drawer of similarly useful objects which might come in handy one day. They never will, but don't let that stop you.

watched as the current carried him away. Miriam ran along the river bank, trying to see where the basket was going. It dodged between fishing boats and under the lines of anglers. Once or twice she thought the waves from passing ships

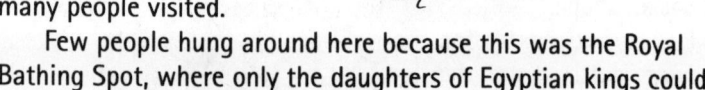

would submerge the basket, but it always seemed to bob up again and eventually it got stuck amongst the reeds in a secluded inlet which not many people visited.

Few people hung around here because this was the Royal Bathing Spot, where only the daughters of Egyptian kings could go to swim. A site safe from prying eyes and the intrusive questions of the Papyrus-razzi.

The princess was just going to dip her toe into the water to test the temperature when she saw the basket. What could it be? Somebody's picnic hamper? A mobile home for ducks? A safe place for a Hebrew baby, created by a mother desperate to save the life of her child? Strangely, none of these ideas passed through her head, which was a pity really. If they had, she would have been so pleased with herself moments later, when she took the lid off the basket.

14

She was about to wade out into the water to explore more, when she suddenly thought, 'I'm a princess. What's the point of having all these maids, servants and under-flunkies if you can't make use of them

at time like this?' So she called one of the girls over and sent her to get the basket.

Miriam watched as her little brother was lifted into the air by the princess. She didn't throw him into the river as Miriam had seen the Egyptian soldiers do to so many other babies. No, the princess seemed delighted, thrilled even. An idea began to take shape in Miriam's mind. She crept out from her hiding place. The royal maids tutted and muttered to themselves. 'Honestly, you find a quiet spot, a place to be alone for a while, and suddenly the place is swarming with babies and children. If you can't go for a bit of a swim these days without this kind of thing happening what is the world coming to?'

'I could find someone to look after the baby for you,' Miriam heard herself saying. The idea appealed to the princess. This way she could have all the pleasure of being a mother, without any

15

of the hard work. The deal was done, and in the first recorded evidence of a child benefit system, the princess even offered to *pay* Miriam's mother for the privilege of bringing up her own baby. (It's a funny old world, innit?)

When he was older and had gone through all the difficult phases of growing up – girls, spots, girls – the princess had him back to live with her in the Palace. Now he needed a name.

The princess thought long and hard about this. It had to say something about the way he was found. There should be the reminder of her stooping into the river to pull out the basket (even though she hadn't... who was going to know that? Princesses could always claim the credit, even if they did none of the work. It was in their job description). The name could be a play on words, reminding others that the basket came out of the river, and the baby came out of the basket. So she gave him a name which means 'Drawn out' (a bit like this explanation). She called him

MOSES.

2 MOSES DOES A RUNNER

EXODUS 2:11-16

As Pharaoh had realised years before, babies grow into men. (Well, male babies do anyway – Pharaoh was cruel, not stupid.) So it was that Moses became part of the royal household. A prince by adoption. Pharaoh welcomed him: this young man was not a threat, why he was practically 'one of them'. If he'd known then what we know now, things would have been so different, and this book would have been so much shorter.

The Hebrews had dreamed of being free. Their ancestors had been promised they would have their own land. Now all they had to look forward to each day was hours of back-breaking labour, as the Egyptians forced them to build their cities, and paid them very little (if anything). At night they would crawl back to their homes – bruised, battered and broken, and dream of a hero.

17

They wanted an action man. Unfortunately, Moses was more of a 're-action man'. He did things first and thought about them later. Cowboys of the Wild West, who adopted a lifestyle of 'shoot first, ask questions later', probably had Moses as their role model. For example, take this incident when there was a breakdown in management/worker relations...

Moses was out inspecting the building works. As he looked in the eyes of the slaves, he saw pain and misery. If he looked for too long he would remember that once he had been part of their nation. Now in his fine robes and expensive jewellery, who would think he'd ever had anything to do with them? Strange really, one basket-ride down the river and everything had changed. For him at any rate.

With these thoughts running round his head, he saw an Egyptian beating one of the slaves. Moses, as I mentioned earlier, just reacted. He didn't take the Egyptian on one side for a little talk. He didn't issue a royal warning to the man. He just killed him, buried him and went on his way. This would have been all well and good, but there is an important lesson in life that everybody has to learn sooner or later. If you are going to get involved in fighting, murder and hiding the body, and you want to get away with it, remember this:

IT IS VERY IMPORTANT NOT TO BE FOUND OUT.

And he had been.

The following day, he saw two Hebrews fighting and, reacting again, he tried to come between them. 'And if we don't stop,' said one, 'I suppose you'll kill us too, just like the Egyptian.'

Moses gulped. The word was out. Palace favourite or not, there was going to be trouble when Pharoah found out. Which he did, and there was.

Re-action Man did the only sensible thing. He was too big to get back into the basket and sail off down the river. So he ran – not West like the cowboys he was to inspire in a future age – but East, through the desert, beyond the Red Sea and into Midian.

It was hot in Midian. Moses sat exhausted by the well, jumping at every noise. Would the Egyptian palace SAS find him out this far? Being a fugitive was no fun. Moses didn't know whether it was safe to stay where he was, or whether he should 'leave well alone' and move on. Then he heard a noise. He moved to the shelter of a nearby rock and watched as people approached.

Unless the armed guards were now recruiting women, and using sheep and goats as undercover agents, it looked like he was safe. Some women – seven sisters – were coming to water their flock. As they got close to the well, the local chapter of 'Hell's Shepherds' appeared to warn them off. They could have some water, said the shepherds. But you don't get anything for nothing in this life so what was in it for them? That's what they wanted to know. The sisters huddled together. They weren't quite sure what the shepherds meant, but they suspected that they weren't about to be invited round for tea.

Before anyone knew what was happening, old Reaction Man was off again. We don't know what he did, but the shepherds just turned and ran, wagging their tails behind them.

What a sight Moses must have been, shooting out from behind the rock – sunburned, hair matted with sand and dirt, his tattered royal robes billowing out behind him, and an aroma suggesting that baths had not been on the agenda for some time. No wonder the shepherds fled.

The women watched as this – whatever or whoever he was – took the goats and sheep and let them have their fill of water. Then the seven sisters went home, eager to tell their father Jethro of this 'Weird Well Warrior and his Wonderful Ways'.

Jethro was made of more down to earth stuff. 'Why didn't you ask him for tea?' he demanded. The girls ran back to the well. The Weird Well Warrior was still there. Moses came back with them, had a wash and brush-up, and stayed for dinner. Then he stayed the night. After that, he stayed for a few more days. Days turned into weeks, months and even years. Moses became part of the family. He married one of the sisters and worked in the family business, looking after the flocks and herds. And they all lived happily ever after...

Er, not quite.

It would have been easy to settle down and talk of the days in Egypt as part of a different life, but something in Moses' heart kept reminding him of a people who were suffering. It was hard to believe he could just turn his back on them and join this new family and tribe. They were known as Midianites and jolly nice people too, as far as Moses knew. The point was, he'd only just found the courage to take the side of his own people, the Hebrews, and even if he applied for Midianite citizenship, he would always know that he belonged elsewhere. It was not easy being the outsider – he'd had a lifetime of it. As he was growing up in the palace, he had sometimes heard whispers and giggles while he walked down the corridor: 'The princess' pet'; 'Little upstart'; 'Hebrew the Sheep-

22

poo'. Those were the kind of things that people said. In Midian, nobody was so rude, but on quiet nights Moses' thoughts would go back to slave camps and the faces of his suffering people. That's where he really belonged.

Moses made his feelings plain when his wife, Zipporah, had a baby boy who they called 'Gershom'. The name meant 'foreigner', and as the family watched the baby grow, they knew that Moses had given them a clear message: he wouldn't be around for ever.

Meanwhile, back in Egypt, Pharoah was dead, but the new Pharoah kept the old traditions going. Slavery, torture, killing babies – you know, the usual stuff. The Hebrew people needed help. Fortunately for them, God – who hasn't been mentioned so far – had not forgotten them.

It was time for Reaction Man to start to become... (drum roll please) ACTION MAN!

Moses looked around. Everything seemed fairly normal. The sun was hot (well, it always is), the desert was sandy (well...) and the sheep were... smelly (you get the idea?).

A few yards away a bush burst into flames. Moses didn't even blink. Here on the slopes of Sinai that kind of thing happened all the time. Moses had never heard the phrase 'spontaneous combustion', he certainly couldn't spell it, but he knew it when he saw it.[3] Just another day in Midian. Moses turned to look at the sheep and did a quick count.

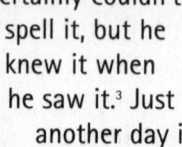

After all these years, he still counted in Egyptian, and he had just got to:

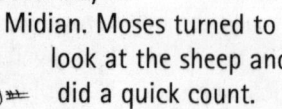 (thirty-four and a half)

when the inevitable happened (you try counting sheep), and apart from the sheep all that could be heard was:

When he woke up, it all looked the same. Same sun, same sand,

---

[3] You can see this happening in the desert to this day. If you should happen to come across such a bush – listen carefully.

24

same sheep, another bush burning. Moses looked again. It was the same bush. Moses looked again. Yes, it was definitely the same bush, but nothing had actually been burned, although the fire was raging. This needed looking into. Moses walked nearer to the bush which suddenly said, 'Moses'. He kept his cool, he was not going to get overheated just because a burning bush had started talking to him. 'I'm here,' he said. Not the most brilliant of replies but, to

be honest, the Egyptian education system had not spent a lot of time on 'Things to say when talking to a bush (burning or otherwise)'. Still, 'I'm here,' was short and to the point – no beating about the bush.

The bush sizzled again. 'Take your shoes off.' Moses slipped off his sandals, wondering if he had been out in the sun too long. The bush carried on burning and it carried on speaking:

'This is a holy place and I am the God of your ancestors.'

Moses thought about this. Which god of his ancestors? There were so many: Khons the moon god; Isis, goddess of women; Sobek the crocodile god; Hathor, the goddess of love. Moses was running through the list in his head, and at the same time was vaguely aware of the bush talking about 'Abraham, Isaac and Jacob'. Suddenly the lights went on – however you want to put it – Moses knew what the bush was talking about. *That* God! *The* God! It was very confusing given his upbringing, but this was to do with his *real* ancestors and the God *they* worshipped. The God they called 'Elohim: Almighty, Strength, All-Powerful, Creator'. The God he had heard the slaves in the work camps crying out to. Why had God come all this way to find him? It felt like trouble, just when everything was so settled. The bush was still burning and still speaking.

'I know about their suffering and I am going to rescue them.'

JACOB   ABRAHAM   ISAAC

('Good news,' thought Moses, 'but why tell me?')
'I will give them their own land full of good things.'
('Marvellous, but what has this got to do with me?')
'I want you to tell Pharoah they have to be set free.'
('Uh-oh.')

Now, apart from being a wanted man in Egypt and the petrifying thought of thousands of Hebrews actually listening to him, Moses thought he was going to look a bit silly just turning up and saying, 'A bush has sent me to rescue you'.

'Say "I AM" sent you,' said the bush.

Moses thought, on balance, he'd rather say a bush had sent him. But the bush was clear.[4]

'I was who I was, I am who I am, I will be who I will be. I do not doze. I am the same God today as I was yesterday and will be tomorrow. The God they have called out to has heard them and he *will* rescue them.'

This was all well and good, but Moses still had to do the 'going' and the 'telling' and, well, quite honestly, he wasn't up to it. He wasn't a good speaker. As he explained to the bush, he couldn't put words together in their correct grammatical and syntactical order, generally finding himself on both public and private occasions unable to articulate in a manner designed to communicate clearly and effectively, thus enabling a sufficient understanding to be swiftly reached by those gathered and desirous of being cognisant of what it was that the speaker was attempting to convey.

It was, all things considered, one of the most eloquent speeches the sheep had heard for a long time. They were impressed, but the bush was not going to be put off.

---

[4] Obviously, when I say 'clear', I mean that the bush knew what it was talking about, not that it was made of glass.

27

When the bush turned Moses' stick into a snake, he began to realise he couldn't explain this one away as being just another bad dream. Moses thought maybe, just maybe, this really was God talking to him. When Moses looked at his hand and found that he'd contracted some unsightly skin disease (scabby skin, oozing pus, flaky bits, the lot), which disappeared as soon as he put his hand in his shepherd's smock, he couldn't really argue any more. But he tried one last time.

'Couldn't you send someone else?'

God decided that if Moses wanted a helper, he could have one. It would mean going back to the Hebrew slave camps in Egypt and searching for his older brother Aaron (remember him?). A bit of a bother, but God didn't see why Moses shouldn't put himself out a bit, since he was the one creating the difficulties. Aaron could go and do the speaking for him, but Moses still had to go and, using the stick/snake and skin disease tricks, show Pharoah that God was a God who meant business.

3 MISSION IMPOSSIBLE

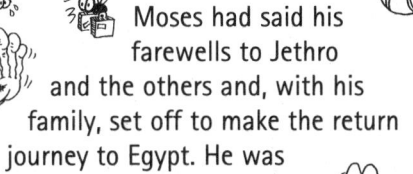

EXODUS 4:18–5:21

Moses had said his farewells to Jethro and the others and, with his family, set off to make the return journey to Egypt. He was afraid of what lay ahead, but also relieved that his brother would be with him. Just one problem though. How, amongst all those thousands of slaves, would he find Aaron?

God, of course, had thought of everything, and before Moses had travelled too far, he was aware of someone coming towards him. Was it some Egyptian agent who had been sent out to look for him? As the figure drew closer, Moses realised he was wearing the wrong sort of clothes – Hebrew style, not Egyptian. Well, maybe this person would be able to advise him on the best way of searching for his brother.

'Oh,' said the Hebrew, when he drew level with Moses. 'I think I can help you there. In fact, if you look straight ahead you should see him.'

'But all I can see is you,' said Moses.

29

'That's right,' said the man... well, you know who it was don't you? It took Moses a little longer for the penny to drop, but drop it did, with a clang that could be heard from one end of the desert to the other.

What a party they had, as these family members were reunited. But there was a time when the partying had to stop. There was a job to do and it could wait no longer.

Together, they went to the Hebrew leaders. Aaron did the talking, and Moses threw down his stick and told the people to put their hands in their coats and take them out again.

Not much in itself, but it's amazing how persuasive snakes and diseases suddenly appearing can be.

Now the biggest hurdle lay ahead – persuading Pharoah. Moses and Aaron approached the palace gates and rang the doorbell (the usual Egyptian kind of bell which played Greensleeves). Moses and Aaron told

Pharoah that God had sent them, and he was to let the Hebrew people go out into the desert to worship him. Pharoah listened politely, considered the request for all of five seconds, and then said 'No'. No debate. No discussion. He was the king round here and he was not going to start listening to every Tom, Dick and Aaron who got some bee in their bonnet about equal rites and equality of opportunity. In fact, if they'd had time to think about such things, obviously life was too easy for the Hebrews. So Pharoah ordered the straw to be taken away from the slaves (an essential ingredient in their brick-making work), but still insisted they make the required number of bricks each day. This meant getting up even earlier to find their own straw. It was an impossible task. The more they tried, the harder it became. The fewer bricks they made, the more they were whipped. The people knew who to blame for all this (and it wasn't the Egyptians). Life had been tough before Moses and Aaron started stirring things up, but at least there were fewer beatings and you got a bit more sleep.

Now the Hebrews turned on these two troublemakers. Thoughts of God punishing Pharoah had vanished. What they wanted was to see God deal with these two, so that they could get back to their bricks.

31

Moses felt sorry for himself and he told God all about it.

'I've left my family and my job. I came to offer help, and look at all the thanks I get. Pharoah hates me, the Hebrews hate me, I don't even like myself very much. And another thing – how come *I'm* the one getting all the aggro? This was your idea, not mine, and you haven't done a single thing.'

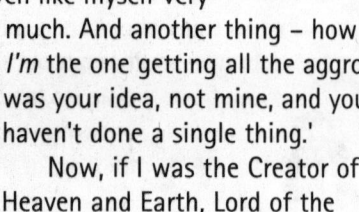

Now, if I was the Creator of Heaven and Earth, Lord of the Universe and somebody had spoken to me like that, I would have blitzed him with thunderbolts left, right and centre. God, however, doesn't work like that. He had his plans and things would work out. He explained patiently and clearly to Moses in words of one syllable:

'I will do it. They will be free. The land is theirs. He will not win. I am the Lord. Now if you have got that in your head, can I please go back to long words? To speak like this is not ease...y.' (D'OH'!)

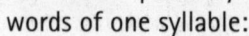

Moses told the people all this, but they were too tired, their backs hurt and they were bricking it. All they could think about was the next day, and getting through it. They hadn't time for dreams of a new

32

EXODUS 7:8 – 10:29

land and freedom. Moses got the message – 'Please just leave us alone.' God, however, was not going to give up. If he said he was going to do something, then he did it. He sent Moses and Aaron to try reasoning with Pharaoh once more. They even did the stick/snake trick for him. He just laughed and got his court magicians to do the same. He soon shut up, though, when Aaron's snake ate all the others, but he was not about to change his mind.

'Well,' thought God, 'we'll see about that.' The next stage of his plan was ready. There would be disaster for the people of Egypt. The longer Pharaoh said the Hebrews could not leave, the worse it was going to get.

And so the plagues began...
It was bad enough when the River Nile turned to blood. It wasn't just the stench of dead fish and the absence of drinking water – you couldn't get your washing done, and so there were no clean shirts and pants to wear on a Friday night. Pharoah, however, just stamped his foot and refused to listen.

Then came the frogs – millions of them. In the food, in the beds, in your cornflakes, down your trousers, staring up from the toilet bowl, sitting on your doorstep, pouring over the chariots, waiting to leap out round corners with that incessant 'Ribbit, ribbit' all day and all night. Moses didn't want to say, 'I toad you so,' but Pharoah had been warned. In the end, he gave in, and said that as soon as the frogs had gone, Moses and Aaron could go and take the people to make sacrifices to their God. The frogs died and lay across the land, reminding everyone who walked outside and heard the squelch and crunch underfoot just what had happened. In the heat of the sun the smell of rotting frog was everywhere, and back then no one had thought of eating the legs. But as far as Pharaoh was concerned, the smell was better than the 'Ribbit', so he changed his mind. 'You can't take them after all,' he told Moses. (The people that is, not the frogs – they weren't going anywhere.)

So God continued the onslaught. It was gnats and flies next, who soon got tired of feeding on dead frogs, and went for live Egyptians instead. They say 'time's fun when you're having flies' (ahem), but the Egyptians didn't think so. Even the palace magicians, who so far had managed to keep up by using their skills to reproduce the effects, couldn't cope any more. 'This is God,' they told Pharoah, but he wasn't listening.

He was not just plagued by flies, he was plagued by people demanding every day that he *do* something. But what could *he* do? If the slaves had their day trip to go and worship, what were the chances of them coming back?

He tried to negotiate with Moses. 'Couldn't they worship their God in Egypt?'
'Oh yes, very likely,' said Moses. 'And I suppose as soon as we start, we'll have Egyptians attacking us and disrupting everything? Look which part of "Let us go" don't you understand? We go, the flies go. Simple.'

Once again, Pharoah agreed, and sure enough the flies vanished. But as quickly as they disappeared, so did his promise. 'I've changed my mind.' That's all you need to say when you're Pharoah.

So it continued. Once again God showed his power, as the Egyptian livestock started to drop dead. Then the people and the animals that were left broke out in boils – not a pretty sight. But that was OK, because the next thing that happened was the worst storm in Egypt's history and what with the thunder, the rain and the enormous hailstones, you couldn't see anybody anyway.

Moses had been getting more and more confident in God, and was now doing more of the talking. He prayed for the storm to stop. It did. But not before the crops had been destroyed. The Hebrews could practically stop the brick production now there was going to be no grain to store in the cities they were building.

The palace officials wanted Pharoah to do something. He was their king and he just wasn't coming up to scratch. Well, not since the boils anyway, but that was another matter. Pharoah was still worried about losing his entire workforce if the Hebrews were allowed to leave. Eventually, after much persuasion, more threats from Moses and Aaron, he said the Hebrews could go... but only the men. He knew full well that, as long as he had their families, the dads would return. This was not good enough...

As the Egyptians gazed at their ruined farm lands, rubbed the parts where they could still feel the sores, and thought about all the animals they had lost, they could hear a faint humming in the distance. The humming became a buzzing, which turned into a drone and then a rumble. The rumble became a cacophony of noise, louder than they had ever heard, and as the noise grew louder the sky grew blacker. There was a noisy black cloud heading straight for them. More rain? More storms? It couldn't be more gnats and flies because there was nothing in Egypt left to bite – the livestock was dead and the Egyptians had got pretty handy with their fly-swatters... but it seemed no one had told *the locusts* about any of this. The Egyptians thought the land had been devastated before, but now it was completely destroyed.

By the time the locusts had moved on, there was no food, no livestock, the river was still unfit to drink from, the roads were littered with dead bodies of all kinds and, to top it all, the people didn't feel well.

Pharoah was not going to change his mind. After all, it couldn't get any worse, could it? The sky turned dark now, not with locusts but with a permanent night. The darkness of the night was really dark, a *dark* kind of darkness they had never known before (this is sounding suspiciously like an annoying washing powder commercial). The people felt dark inside and out. Life could not go on like this.

Pharoah had had enough. He threw Moses out of the palace with threats and curses. He was not going to let the Hebrews go. But if Pharoah thought it was dark now... he had no idea how black things would really get.

4 FREE AT LAST

The Egyptians were afraid. What would happen next? How would they survive? Could nobody deal with the Hebrews? And didn't ANYONE have a good treatment for boils? These were the sort of questions that were going through their minds. Clearly, Moses was a man to be reckoned with, and if they had to pay him to leave, they'd bring the gold and silver by the barrow-full.

Moses went back to Pharoah. This time he wasn't asking, he was telling. 'We're going, whether you want us to or not, and you'll know when the time comes because your son will be dead. Your first-born, the one who is going to inherit all your wealth, power and position, won't be there. It's all been for nothing and you brought it on yourself.'

It would have been easy for Moses to rub Pharoah's nose in it (whatever 'it' is – use your imagination), but he didn't feel like that. He knew that it wasn't just the king's son who would die, but the first-born son of every Egyptian in the land. People still shuddered when they remembered the noise of the locusts covering the land, but it would be nothing compared to the cries of sadness at God's last dreadful act. The Israelites would at last be free, but it would be at a high cost for the Egyptians, and for Pharoah.

39

'Pack up,' said Moses to the people of Israel, 'we're going.' The people sighed and muttered, and some even grumbled a bit. They had heard it all before and every time, just when the final donkey was loaded and they were jumping on their suitcases to shut the lids, Pharaoh changed his mind. However, one or two looked at Moses' face – there was a sadness and weariness about his eyes. This time it was different. This time it could really be true. There were arrangements to make, sorting out and getting ready. The date to mark in red on the calendar was the tenth. It wasn't the only thing to be marked in red, but we'll come to that later.

God had plans for a final meal. A farewell supper of lamb or goat roasted with herbs and flat tasteless bread. There were those who thought something a bit more special was called for. Some of the more enterprising Hebrew chefs began thinking of goat's cheese tartlets in filo pastry parcels with a medley of spring vegetables perhaps washed down with some of the local tipple (Chateau de Nile). However, one look at Moses' face told them that this was not a time for elaborate meals and ten course dinners. The meal was to be eaten when all the packing was done – when God gave the word they had to go. No hanging about for second courses and a look at the cheese board. Then there was all that business with the blood...

The animal's blood, whether goat or lamb, had to be painted on the doorposts. The blood was a sign to God that these people were to be protected. Of course, the blood could also drip down the neck of the next person to walk through the doorway slowly, but no matter. 'When I see the blood I will pass over your houses,' said the Lord God. So it was that ever afterwards, when the descendants of the people of Israel ate the meal to remember this incredible night, they called it the 'Passover' festival. This was lucky – just think, if God had chosen to talk of it in another way, Jews today could be sitting down once a year to the 'I'm just nipping over to the Egyptians to sort them out, make sure you're ready to leave when I come back' festival, which would have been a bit of a mouthful (and less digestible than the goat).

The preparations were ready. The blood was on the doorposts, the families were all gathered inside with their herby-goat sandwiches in their hands, waiting for the word. The silence was loud enough to fill the empty land. People breathed only when they had to, and still they waited.

Finally, at midnight, in an Egyptian house nearest the Hebrew camp, came a cry that split the silence of the night like a thunderbolt. A cry of desolation and despair that caused the people of Israel to shiver. Then there was an echoing cry from further away. And more and more. Soon the night silence was filled with the cries and tears of a nation. A nation that had refused to listen to God until it was time for the talking to stop.

In the palace Pharoah turned from the dead body of his son and, with tears still streaming down his face, sent for Moses and Aaron.

'Go,' he said to them. 'Go now. Go quickly.'

Moses and Aaron spread the word and the Israelites were on the move, helped by hundreds of Egyptians who came to make sure they went, before anything worse could happen. Although at this particular moment it was difficult to imagine what *could* be worse.

So the Israelites walked free. It had been 430 years since Joseph had brought his father Jacob and his family to the land. Almost 400 years since Joseph had promised the people, with his dying breath, 'God will come to your rescue'. And Joseph had been right. It had taken longer than many thought, and some believed it would never come, but it had. God had kept his promises. If you looked carefully amongst the six hundred thousand men and countless women and children pouring over the Egyptian border, as well as the blankets and clothes and animals and cooking pots, you would have seen four people carrying a box. An old box, but it was being carried with care and respect, despite the urgent mood of the night. In the box were the bones of Joseph, the one who had promised their rescue all those years ago. Moses had made sure that, on this night of all nights, he would be rescued too.

And there, at the front of them all, was a huge column of fire, showing the way through the darkness. In the day, the fire became a cloud, and whether they saw cloud or fire, whatever the time, the people knew that God their rescuer was also going to be their guide into the future he had planned.

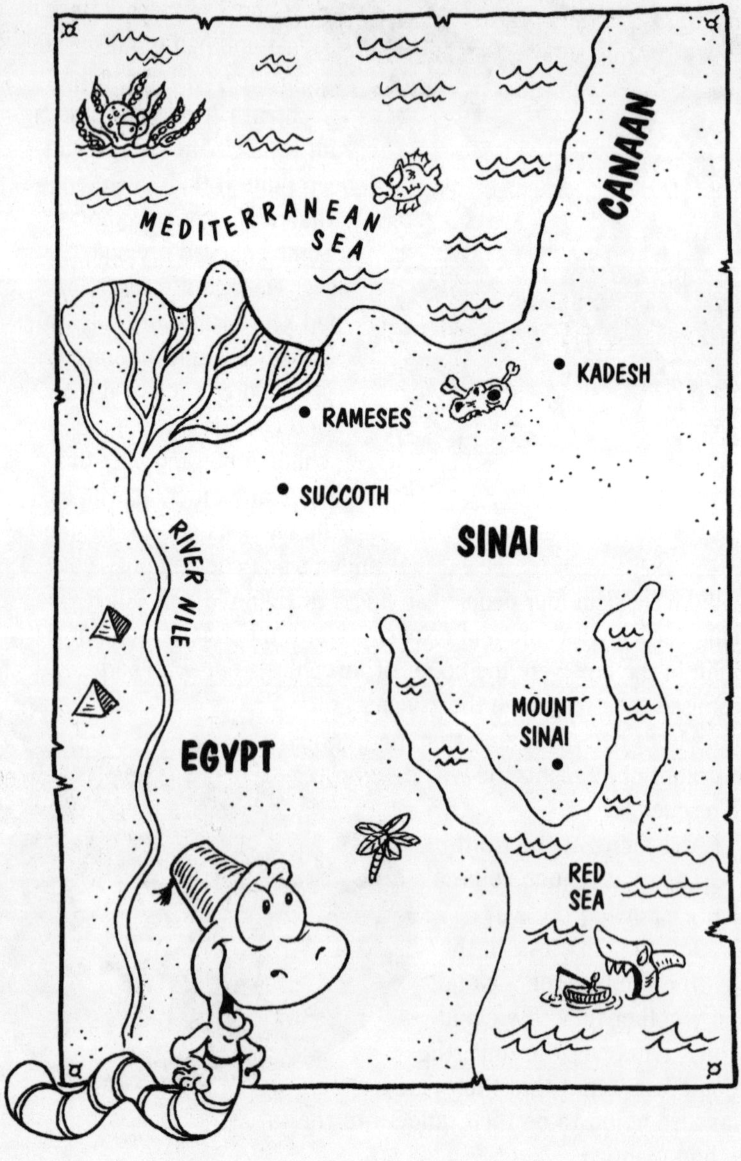
MEDITERRANEAN SEA
CANAAN
KADESH
RAMESES
SUCCOTH
SINAI
RIVER NILE
MOUNT SINAI
EGYPT
RED SEA

'What're we going this way for?' asked a voice in the crowd. There's always someone on any journey who knows better. 'If we'd turned right at that last junction we could have cut this corner, avoided the hold-ups by the building site, and missed out Succoth altogether, 'cos you know what the traffic is like there this time of day. Then it would have been straight on through Megiddo, slow down through the speed traps and Mesopotamia and Bob's your uncle. And by the way, I can see the sea and I need the loo.' The person next to him (who by a strange coincidence *did* have an uncle called Bob) begged to differ. 'You could go that way, yes, but there was always problems with the Philistines that way, and quite honestly I haven't come all this way just to become part of a kebab on a Philistine spear!' The debate went on, but fortunately God was chief navigator, and he was going the way he wanted to go, straight through the sea.

As it dawned on the people where they were going, they fell silent again. Some checked their luggage for inflatable dinghies, rubber rings and scuba-diving equipment – but they weren't there.

EXODUS 12:37–15:21

'YOU NEVER SAID YOU COULDN'T SWIM'

'ALL THESE YEARS I'VE JUST BEEN IN DE-"NILE"'

45

Hardly surprising, as they weren't due to be invented for several thousand more years. 'But I haven't packed my trunks,' said one voice. 'More to the point, I can't swim,' he added after a few moments thought.

The people came to the sea and stopped. They couldn't go forward and behind them, if they were not mistaken, was the distant rumble of Egyptian chariots. Clearly, Pharoah was out for revenge, and judging by the clouds of dust on the horizon, he was bringing most of the Egyptians with him.

The people turned on Moses. This was not what they'd expected. Freedom yes, but freedom for ever, not for the few hours it took Pharoah and his army to catch up with them. 'Don't worry,' said Moses. 'Be brave. God will save us.' This was quite impressive, because inside he was thinking something which roughly translates as 'Heeeeeeeeeeeeeee eeeeeeeeeeeeeeeelp!'

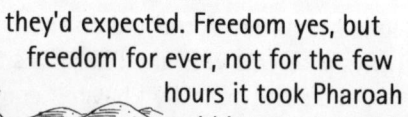

'Trust me,' said God to Moses, 'and go and hold your stick over the waters of the sea.' Now Moses had seen God do some

46

pretty impressive things, but even he wasn't convinced that the stick/snake trick was going to do the business this time. It was just as well, then, that God had something else in mind. As Moses went towards the water everything went dark behind him, just like back in Egypt during those dark days of dark darkness. Over where the Israelites were, though, it was as bright as a sunny day in sunshine land in the summer (and that's bright). The Egyptians ground to a halt. They couldn't see where they were going. Surely, it would be better to wait for this freak cloud to pass over... well 'pass by' (Passover was not a word the Egyptians were ever going to use again if they could help it).

Moses held out his stick and the wind began to blow. It blew harder and faster. Moses blinked and looked again. Where had the sea gone? He looked at Aaron with the 'What *is* going on now?' expression that his brother had got so used to over recent months. Aaron grabbed his arm. 'I've no idea bro' but let's get moving and whatever you do, keep that stick in the air.' They walked forward, the land was dry. The people followed, trying not to look at the huge walls of water on either side. They didn't understand it, and they couldn't believe it, but the time for arguing about it would come later. For now, they just wanted to get across. At the other side they looked back. They could see the whole Egyptian army trying to follow them across the sea bed, but without four wheel-drive, the chariots found the mud pretty heavy going.

47

'Now,' said the Lord, 'hold your stick over the water again, Moses.' By now, Moses had had a huge confidence injection and didn't need telling twice. Up went the stick, down came the waters with such force and speed that soon, wherever there had been Egyptians, there were now just empty chariots and bodies floating face down in the water.

Moses looked round at his people. Not one was looking at him. They were down on their knees, telling God in their own words, in hundreds of different ways, that he was God – truly God – and they would like to do things his way, if that was all right with him.

Then the singing began, with Moses providing a tuneful lead, in a not unattractive baritone voice, and Miriam (who had watched that basket float down the Nile all those years ago) leading the Hebrew Ladies Tambourine Chorus and Dance Troupe[5]. The song went something like this:

---

[5] Available for Barmitzvahs, weddings and end of term parties.

**GOD'S WON!
THE EGYPTIANS DROWNED!
GOD'S COOL!
THE EGYPTIANS ARE TERMINALLY WET IN A RED SEA SWIMMING POOL!
O, GOD YOU ARE THE BEST!
YO, GOD!**

Admittedly it loses something in the translation, but you get the idea.

5 MOANING, MANNA AND MIRACLES

NUMBERS 20:1-13

EXODUS 15:22-17:7

In the desert there was a rumbling and a grumbling. The Israelites looked to the skies but there was no sign of locusts; they looked to the horizon, yet not a hint of an Egyptian chariot; but the rumbling continued. It was the people – stomachs churning away for food and water, and everyone standing around thinking of how much nicer slavery was. Yes, there had been torture – but grain and figs to follow and grapes for dessert. Now here they were in the desert and the only water they could find had the foulest taste imaginable. In fact, they named the place 'Marah' which means 'bitter', as a warning to any other escaped slaves who might pass that way. But God had not brought them this far just to let them die of thirst. So when Moses asked him to help, he told Moses to throw a lump of wood into the water. 'Well,' thought Moses, 'it can't make it taste worse.' He was right – it didn't. In fact, it tasted a whole lot better. The people rushed to the waterside, drinking their fill, slaking their thirsts, quenching their parched throats. Suddenly, all the complaining

> THIS WATER TASTES LIKE BARLEY-WATER
>
> WEE IN THE WATER AND THERE'LL BE TROUBLE!

had vanished and all that could be heard were cries of, 'Lovely', 'Fill the water bottles' and 'Because I'm worth it!' and the occasional splash when somebody leaned over too far.

When the people had had their fill, God reminded them who had saved them from Egypt, who had kept them safe through the Red Sea, and who had provided the water. He then made them a promise – 'I have proved I care for you in a variety of ways,' said God. 'Now my care will continue for ever if you stay with me, do the things I tell you and learn from me as you travel on.' This seemed like a good deal, and the people were keen to agree but, of course, although they had their fill of water, there was still the question of 'What's for breakfast?' (and lunch, dinner, tea, supper and all those little in-between snacks).

God, who hadn't let them down so far, was not about to start now. 'There will be food,' he promised, 'and there will be enough for everyone. Meat at night and bread in the morning.' The people looked round for a delivery van, or sign of a local deli serving fresh salt-beef bagels but, apart from those who had been out in the sun too long, nobody saw a thing.

'EXCUSEZ-MOI! EST-CE QU'IL Y A UNE BOULANGERIE PRES D'ICI?'

51

Suddenly, the air was full of quails plummeting from the sky. Quails are tiny birds, but the meat was considered a great delicacy. The people rushed around scooping up quail meat from all over the place, and that night everybody had just enough to fill their stomachs. Somebody was overheard picking up his quail and muttering about it not being ready-cooked, but some people are never satisfied.

QUAIL BURGER

QUAIL, PRUNES AND CUSTARD

The next morning, the people looked out of their tents and stared at the snow – not a common occurrence in the desert. Then they looked again and realised it only *looked* like snow. Of course they could see now it was... well, what was it? A sort of flaky, frosty thing (unlike frosted flakes, which are something completely different and wouldn't be invented for thousands of years). Somebody eventually picked a bit up. He licked it carefully. It tasted like, well, like a flaky, frosty, kind of bread. When the rest

EARLY VARIATION ON THE SNOW PLOUGH

52

of the people saw that he hadn't dropped down dead, and that he seemed to quite like the stuff, they suddenly became very brave and collected it by the basket load. Of course, they had to decide what to call it. 'Flaky, frosty thing which fell out of the sky and tastes like bread' was a bit of a mouthful (just like the stuff itself), so they decided to call it 'What is it?', since that is what most people had said when they saw it. In their language the word for 'what is it?' is 'manna', and so manna it was. The people soon cleared the ground of the food (because manna hands make light work!) and all the families had their fill.

Once again, God had proved that he could be trusted, but he wanted the people to show they trusted him. So he told them only to collect enough food for what they needed that day. There should be no picking up extra and storing it at the back of the tent 'just in case'. This would demonstrate that the people believed God would continue to provide food, day after day.

Of course, there were some who thought it was better to be safe than sorry, but they ended up just being sorry. Some did collect too much, but they found the next day that it had gone mouldy and was full of worms which, even as a change from quail, weren't that appealing. However, there was one day when they *were* allowed to collect more. On Fridays they could take double the amount. That way, they would already have food for the Sabbath and so could rest, as God has always wanted people to.

So it went on for forty years, by the end of which time the book *Desert Entertaining with Manna and Quail* could have been a best-seller. It would certainly have been more in demand than the less well-known title *Manna and Quails Entertaining Desserts* book.

The people were thirsty again. The food was turning up every day, just like God had promised, but they were feeling a bit dry. Once again, it was Moses and Aaron who had to field the complaints. Knowing they couldn't sort it out by themselves, they went to God for help. He told Moses to get his old stick out. After the incident at the Red Sea, Moses didn't really think there was enough water to gargle with, let alone... However, he was beginning to learn that God's way may not be our way, and that he probably knows best. So he got the stick and God told him to hit the rock that was nearby.

While the people watched with their tongues hanging out (not with wonder and amazement – they were just thirsty), Moses lifted his stick and brought it crashing down onto the rock once, as God had said, and once more to make sure. The people waited, but not for long, as water gushed out of the rock soaking everybody around. The complaining disappeared (although the area would be known as 'Meribah' – 'the grumbling place' ever afterwards), and everybody was happy... well, almost everybody.

God was not pleased, and wanted a little word with Moses and Aaron. 'I said "ONCE",' he thundered at them. 'Hit the rock *once*, not twice. I'm trying to teach the people to trust me, and you have to be the best example there can be. *Once* was enough. You're like those people who go around collecting extra quails, thinking they can store them away for an emergency. Don't you understand? I have promised to be with you – there is no emergency that I cannot deal with – but you and everyone else have *got* to trust me. I have got great plans for this people, and a land waiting for them where they will be able to demonstrate to the world what it means to trust me completely. You, Moses, will take them to that land, but you won't go in. I will find another leader to carry on my work from there.'

'OH-ER! HE'S LOOKING QUITE SHEEPISH'

EXODUS 17:8 – 18:27
DEUTERONOMY 1:9–18

Moses felt really thick. He could have kicked himself (just the once). How could he have been so stupid? He

'THIS DESERT AIN'T BIG ENOUGH FOR THE TWO OF US'

hadn't much time to feel sorry for himself though, as there was so much to do. Not least was having to deal with an army of Amalekites, who had just appeared over the nearest sand dune, and didn't look too happy at having to share the desert with a scruffy looking bunch of slaves from the wrong side of the Red Sea.

The commander of the Hebrew army, Joshua, was on the case and took his group of soldiers into battle. Moses had learned something during the 'water and rock' episode – the only secure way is to let God work things out, and allow him control. This must be as true in war as in peace. It wasn't that Joshua and his men weren't good, it was just that, without God on your side, you might as well surrender and chop off your ... while you're at it, to save the Amalekites time later. So Moses went and stood on a hill, and watched the battle with his arms raised, as a sign of God's blessing and presence with the people. Sure enough, while Moses stood like that the Israelites were winning. If he let his arms drop, the Amalekites started winning. For a whole day he stood like this, and when his arms felt like they would drop off, Aaron and Hur (not Him... Hur) held his arms up for him. When the sun went down, the score was 52-0 for Joshua's army and no penalties.

Peace at last... well, of a kind. Moses didn't know who was more trouble – Amalekite soldiers, or his own people, constantly on at him day and night, expecting him to sort out every little difficulty and problem. 'He's got three of my sheep in his flock'; 'I want to move my tent to a better area of the camp'; 'If his camel tramples over my cooking area once more, I'll really get the hump'. It went on and on with no end in sight. Then, in the middle of all this, his father-in-law turned up. Moses loved Jethro. He could never forget his kindness when he was a lonely fugitive in the desert but, quite honestly, visiting relatives was the last thing he needed. However, Moses was going to have reason to be glad Jethro turned up when he did.

6 TEN TO ONE

Jethro was watching. He didn't want to interfere. Rule 46 in the *Handy Guide to In-law Etiquette* – DON'T INTERFERE. It's the oldest rule in the book. But, in the end, he couldn't stay quiet any longer. 'Look Moses,' he said, as his son-in-law returned from another day of grumbles, groans and niggling nastiness, 'You shouldn't be killing yourself with all this work. Let me help.' Moses stared at Jethro. 'Sorry,' said his father-in-law, 'that didn't come out quite right. What I meant was, I think there's an easier way to deal with this workload.' Moses scooped up a stunned quail from the floor and began to roast it over the fire, listening to Jethro at the same time.

'STUNNED? I WAS SPEECHLESS!'

Nowadays, a plan like Jethro's would be illustrated with flow diagrams, slide shows, flip-charts, video walls, computerised interactive presentation packages and over-use of phrases such as 'contra-production indicators', 'downsizing' and 'I'm sorry, is that my mobile?' All Jethro had was a stick, some sand to draw in and left-over quail. Nevertheless, with a skill normally possessed only by presenters of Blue Peter, he managed to get Moses to grasp the principle of 'delegation' – just because you're in charge it doesn't mean you have to do all the work yourself. Find others you can trust. Give each of them a group of people to look after. Most of the time, they will be able to sort out any problems. Your job will be to keep in touch with the group leaders and offer support, sympathy and summit meetings with quail sandwiches whenever there's a crisis.

It was brilliant, straightforward and Moses couldn't understand why he hadn't thought of it himself. Still, when he shared the idea with the rest of the people, they weren't going to know that, were they?

With Jethro's new system in place, it was time for the old man to go home and leave Moses to get on with things, and get ready for God's next big announcement which was on its way. It wasn't so much round the corner as up the next big hill, which was called Sinai.

It had never been God's
intention that he should just
watch over a collection of
wandering tribes, giving food and
water when they needed it, and
putting them right when things got

EXODUS 19:1 – 31:18

a bit out of hand. He had bigger
plans than that. He hadn't
rescued the people
from Egypt to
leave them in a
desert, with a vague
sense that they were special-in-some-
way-but-they-couldn't-quite-see-how.
God made people to be his friends
– to share their lives with him,
talk to him, and to go through the
good times and bad times together. He wanted the whole world
to know this kind of friendship, and he wanted one group of
people to show the way – his own group of people, doing things
his way.

The last time Moses had been on Sinai, a
bush had spoken
to him. He had
come a long way
since then
(although now he
was back where he
started). This time, as
he climbed the mountain,
he *knew* who he was going
to talk with.

So it was that, alone and
out of sight of the rest of his
people, Moses listened, as God outlined

60

the deal. His mind could hardly take it all in – the Living God, the Lord of the whole earth who had done incredible things in Egypt, who parted the sea so that people could cross safely, and kept them fed and watered, was offering to make them *his* people. In return, all God asked for was obedience. Complete obedience. Total and unswerving obedience. The sort of obedience that meant they did as they were told and didn't ask questions. Obedience where somebody else called the shots. Just like when they were slaves in Egypt... just a minute, that couldn't be right. They had left slavery behind. Surely they weren't going to just swap one tyrant for another? These questions rushed through Moses' head as he imagined what the people would say as he reported back:

'Now listen guys, you know how you used to be slaves back in Pharaoh's place? Well, I've found a Somebody to take his place, so we won't miss the bad old days too much.' This would go down really well – NOT! In fact, Moses could imagine the reaction. It was more likely that HE'D go down really well – the nearest and deepest well they could find.

As Moses listened further, it began to sink into even his slow mind that what God was offering was something completely different. A friendship based on *love*, not fear. Yes, the people would be expected to keep his commands and laws, but they would *choose* to do so. Nobody would *make* them and if they wanted to say 'We'll do things our way' they could (and sadly history was to prove they would – often). In return, God was offering his presence, his protection, his knowledge of how things should be. But if the people were going to go for this, it had to be 100 per cent. This wasn't a computer game they could switch on or off when they felt like it. God was not saying, 'Dress up nice on the Sabbath and do what you like the rest of the time.' He was talking about people choosing, at every moment of every day, in every situation everywhere, to say, 'We belong to the Lord and we will only do the things which please him.' He began to outline what this meant...

It would affect the way they treated slaves and their families, and provide compensation for those injured in arguments.

- Murder was to be treated seriously.
- Pregnant women were to be valued and to be treated as such.
- Animals had to be kept properly, for their own protection and the protection of others.
- Thieves must pay back more than they stole.
- Foreigners coming into the land were to be treated well.
- Widows and orphans had to be cared for.
- Lending money to those in need, and then charging interest and making them suffer more, was not allowed.
- In trials, honesty had to be the keyword.
- Sabbath days were for rest. Their lives were to be marked by celebration. They were to be a people who lived life to the full. Three times a year there would be big festivals, to dance and sing and eat and rejoice, as a sign that the God who they followed was the God of life, not death.

And so the list went on. Moses was desperately trying to

remember it all, but God had thought of that. And so he summed up all he was saying with ten soundbites. A decalogue (if you want to be posh and show off) of short, sharp sentences which, if obeyed, would shape the lives of the Hebrews in the way that they were meant to be shaped, and be a living example to all the nations around. Just ten bullet points, and yet the world ever since has been influenced by them. Countries have formed their laws based on the principles of these instructions. Men and women, when looking for guidelines for life, have turned again and again to these rules, given thousands of years ago. Nowadays, even if people can't tell you what they are individually, most know their overall name. They are of course

THE TEN SUGGESTIONS WHICH YOU CAN TAKE OR LEAVE AS YOU SEE FIT.

Only joking! I mean, of course,

THE TEN COMMANDMENTS

Before I list them for you, why not put this book down for a moment and see how many you can come up with. Use the following scale to grade yourself:

- 0-2: Are you taking this seriously?
- 3-5: Not bad – but don't offer to teach Sunday School just yet.
- 6-8: Getting better – of course knowing them is one thing but do you keep them?
- 9-10: Wow! Are you sure you haven't peeked at the next few pages?
- 11-15: Have you really been paying attention?

And now let's reveal God's Top Ten rules for a happy, holy and highly huplifting life. As you'll see, there's not much movement in the Top Ten this week, with no change in the Top spots. There were those who thought 'Not stealing' might make way for 'Take what you like, just don't get caught', but there are some standards that just aren't up for negotiation. So let's move things along and get straight to the Cosmic Countdown and reveal God's Guidance for a Wandering World.

At number ten: Life is not a self-service restaurant. You can't choose what you want and then, when you see what your friend's got, decide you want some of that as well. Learn to be happy with what you have and laugh at adverts.

I'M HAPPY WITH WHAT I'VE GOT

At number nine: 'Straight up', 'Honestly', 'Cross my heart, hope to die, terrapins tickle me if I lie'. These phrases are out. Just stick to the facts and there won't be any need for all this other stuff – and that's the truth.

At number eight: If you haven't been given it or paid for it, it's not yours so PUT IT BACK, OK?

At number seven: God made marriages to last. Cheating on husbands and wives causes pain, distrust, confusion and anxiety for lots of people, not just two. Those promises you made are meant to be kept.

At number six: Blood is supposed to be on the inside, so keep it there. Life is for living not for ending when somebody irritates us or gets in our way. Murder is out – even a teeny tiny one when nobody is looking. Don't do it – don't even think about it.

At number five: mums and dads – yeah, they're old-fashioned and embarrassing when they try to be trendy, but they've put a lot of time and energy into doing the most difficult job in the world – bringing you up. So how about working with them a little, and not against them. 'Nuff respect, yeah?

At number four: We are not machines. We were meant to have a rest every now and again. About one day off in seven seemed to work for God, so who are we to do any different? Besides, in the rush of a busy week, its easy to forget the big things in life, like who made us, why we're here and the recipe for banana smoothies[6], so one day a week to take time to remember is all part of the plan.

---

[6] See page 68 for more details.

> DAY OF REST MUM! I'LL GO TO THE EVENING SERVICE

At number three: Look, God is God. It's his name, and he is special, so be careful how you use his name. It's not a swearword or an expression of exasperation when you've just lost your favourite Pokèmon card. It's his name – if you use it, don't abuse it.

No change at number two: There is only room for one God in our lives. If we find ourselves thinking about footballers, pop stars, the girl on the number 3 bus or even the Diet Coke man more than God, we've got a problem and should do something about it... NOW!

'LORD I WOULD LISTEN TO YOU MORE IF YOU'D SCORE FOR CITY MORE OFTEN'

Yep, you've guessed it. Still holding on to the number one slot for the fifth millennium in a row is the goldenest of golden rules:

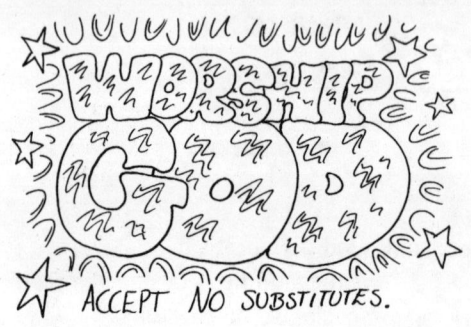

WORSHIP GOD

ACCEPT NO SUBSTITUTES.

DEUTERONOMY 5:1-21

EASY TO MAKE BANANA SMOOTHIES

(but don't forget to ask permission from whoever cleans up the kitchen after you)

You will need:
2 medium bananas
250 ml milk
60 ml of malted milk powder
1 tablespoon of honey
8 ice cubes
1 scoop vanilla ice cream

1 Chop up the bananas.
2 Put all the ingredients in the blender.
3 Switch on blender.
4 Clean up the mess and go back to the beginning. Repeat all the instructions – this time remember to put the lid on the blender.
5 When it's smooth (the clue is in the name), it's ready.

It should make about three lots, so if you have any spare you can e-mail it to me at: dishoftheday@dot.dash.dot.uk

7 THE GOLDEN CULT

As Moses made his way down the mountain to the people below, his mind was full of all that he'd heard, and all that he had to share with Aaron, his Jethro-Inspired Leadership Team Exodus Division and all the others.

The people could see the figure approaching, and they gathered to hear the news. Moses talked of all that God had promised to do for the people – which the crowds all loved. He also told them of all that they had to promise to do in return – which wasn't so exciting, but a deal's a deal when all's said and done.

By the time he had finished, most were nodding in agreement, but one or two had questions. There were those who had got completely confused and were muttering things like 'What have pregnant bulls from another country wanting to borrow money on the Sabbath got to do with me?' (Well, it was a long and detailed list.) Some had fallen asleep, but around the assembled hordes grew a murmur of assent and shouts of 'Let's go for it'.

69

'JUST CHECKING THE SMALL PRINT'

God had already told Moses what the arrangements were if the people wanted to be part of this. It was going to be a big event with seventy-three of the nation's leaders representing the people. There would be sacrifices and a messy ritual involving blood. The people were used to this. It had not been particularly nice smearing blood over their homes on that dark night in Egypt, but they'd seen the results. There was something appropriate about using the very life force in solemn and serious agreements, and on a scale of one to ten this particular agreement scored 139. Moses gathered the blood from the sacrificed animals, and when the people had shouted out long and loud that they would do all that God had commanded, he stood and shouted, 'Let us spray.'

Some of the people misunderstood and were down on their knees with their hands together and eyes closed. Moments later they opened them again as they felt a sprinkling. It was red. Red, and sticky. Red and sticky and it looked a lot like, felt a lot like, was a lot like... blood.

'STRANGE TASTE THIS RAIN'

70

The agreement was signed with blood. The people had chosen to be God's people. The seventy-three leaders went further up the mountain and saw God. The God who was their God. The God who had just agreed to shape and direct their lives for ever.

But there was still more to do, and so God called to Moses to send the people and the leaders away. He wanted to talk to him – there were things he needed to know.

So, as Moses went higher up the mountain, the people returned to their camps, thinking of the incredible day, the ceremony, the majesty, the wonder of it all and, probably wondering how they were going to get the blood out of their clothes.

How long does it take people to forget an unforgettable event like the one the people of Israel had just witnessed on the mountainside? About forty-seven days.

In less time than it takes to read your way through a Sunday paper, all those words of promise and commitment vanished into the wilderness. For, while Moses was learning from God how he was to be worshipped, and of the proof that the people belonged to the Lord alone, down below, those very same people were making their own party plans.

DEUTERONOMY 9:6–29
EXODUS 32:1–35

So it was that, as Moses rejoined the people, carrying his own copy of the Ten Commandments (full two-volume carved stone edition), and thinking if only pockets had been invented, God could have carved them on a pocket-sized version, he stopped, hardly daring to believe what was in front of his eyes.

It was huge; it was golden, with the sun bouncing off its body; it was splendid and magnificent... it was a cow. No, as Moses looked a little closer and remembered his biology lessons, he realised it was a bull-calf. Standing in the centre of the camp. The people were dancing around it, praying to it and offering sacrifices to this lump of shiny metal, sacrifices which belonged to God.

Moses was mad, furious, irate, angry, incensed, pretty cheesed-off. You name it – he was it. It was then that he realised the advantage of having the commandments on two huge bits of stone. Had they been written on a piece of paper, throwing them into the nearest bin would not have had the impact of what he was about to do. He raised the stones above his head and smashed them to the ground, roaring with rage as he did so. The dancing stopped, the singing ended mid-verse, and a young bull about to have its throat cut as a

72

sacrifice escaped, while everyone was staring at Moses.

Suddenly, their decorations seemed cheap, the golden calf was an embarrassment and they all felt very sorry for themselves. How could they have turned their backs on God who had done so much for them? Moses could not believe it. Had they forgotten what it was like back in Egypt? Had they chosen to ignore who it was that was feeding them and keeping them alive? He'd show them. He'd teach them a lesson. He sprang into action, issuing orders for the golden calf to be ground into dust. The dust was poured into the water, and Moses yelled at the people 'Drink it!' Everybody drank – nobody was going to argue with Moses just at the moment. The camp was filled with the sound of coughing and choking.

'I'VE ONLY GOT A NAIL FILE!'

'Now!' yelled Moses. 'Remember the taste of the water at Marah? The bitterness that made you want to vomit?' The people remembered very well, with many of them re-creating the scene before his very eyes. 'Is that what you want to go back to?' shouted Moses. 'Did it mean nothing to you when you agreed to follow the Lord? If you make an agreement and break it, there are consequences – as you are about to find out.' Moses stopped and stared at the people, and out of the corner of his eye was aware of someone slinking away into the crowds. 'Aaron, come back here. I want a word with you.'

His brother turned, and suddenly this great speaker, Moses' right-hand man, the one who had squared up to Pharoah, was at a loss for words. He made some feeble excuse about how the bull had just appeared when he was melting down the gold, but he could tell by the expression on Moses' face that he wasn't buying it.

Moses' next decision was hard, but he knew that if following God was to be taken seriously, hard decisions would sometimes have to be made. He called for those who had been faithful, those who had stayed out of the golden-bull nonsense, to join him. Men from the tribe of Levi came and stood by his side. With a heavy heart, Moses told them what needed to be done. Those who had danced, sung or even contributed a bit of gold to the statue, had betrayed the agreement with God. They had to die. So the Levites rounded up the culprits and, with no sense of pleasure, simply knowing that it was hard to do God's will, put them to death – about three thousand died that day. Their willingness to do even this distasteful job meant that, in future, God was going to trust them with more important jobs.

74

They would be the ones who would lead the people in worship. They would be the constant reminder of all that God wanted them to be and do.

It was time to move on. As God had promised, there was a land waiting for the people of Israel, and Moses had to get them there. There was just one question Moses had. He had been let down by Aaron, so who was going to be with him, to help him on the way now? God's answer was surprising. 'I'll be with you Moses. That's all you need to know.'

Before they packed up camp and set off for this unknown land, there was something else that had to be put right. The people had made a start at being God's unique people, and it had all gone horribly wrong. It was time to start again. God was showing that his desire was to create life, not spread death. More than anything else, he wanted people to share this world with him, and so it was that God gave Moses another set of carved commandments and repeated his promise.

'I promise to perform miracles for you ... Neighbouring nations will stand in fear.' In return, the people had to keep their side of the bargain. The terms hadn't changed.

'I demand your complete loyalty,' said the Lord.

When Moses came back from being with God, his face shining with the light of God, the people listened in silence. They knew how serious the agreement was – some still felt as if they could taste the gold dust in their mouths. It was not a taste they wanted to have again.

8 GOD'S HOUSE

EXODUS 35:4 – 40:38

The Israelites were packed up and ready to go, but Moses had some news for them. They were going to have something extra to carry. The people groaned as they looked at the already over-burdened animals, and their bags, which they'd had to bounce up and down on to get closed. What *else* were they going to have to take?

'A house,' said Moses, 'a home for God.' Until this point the Israelites had got used to God travelling around in a cloud (under his own steam – geddit?) or as fire (blazing a trail... oh, stop it).

'Why the need for a house all of a sudden?' the people wanted to know. This, you will remember, is the same group of people who couldn't let Moses go for a walk in the hills without creating their own religion. Moses explained as patiently as he could: 'It's to make sure you dopes don't ever forget again that God is with us, living with us, walking with us, working with us, just like he promised. Now can you get that into your thick skulls?' Clearly when I say, 'As patiently as he could', I meant, 'Not patiently at all'. Moses described this construction to them. It sounded magnificent. The best metals, the finest cloths, the most brilliant artwork.

'OH IT'S ALL QUITE IN-TENTS!'

76

THE PEOPLE COULD WORK SIX
DAYS LONG,
TO DO ANYMORE WOULD BE
WRONG.
THEY SHOULD WEAR
'SABBATH BEST',
PUT THEIR FEET UP TO REST,
AND WORSHIP THEIR GOD
WITH A SONG.

'But where is all this material going to come from?' was the whisper going round the crowds. As if he could read their thoughts, Moses announced, 'The Lord will provide. In fact, he has already provided.' 'Well that's a relief,' shouted someone from the crowd. 'For a moment we thought you were going to ask us for it.' Moses said nothing, but just smiled quietly. As he stood there, beaming at people, the penny dropped. In fact quite a few pennies dropped – thousands of pounds worth of pennies. Moses didn't have to ask anybody for money. People started to get so excited about what was planned, that they gave almost without thinking. They knew that if they wanted to build God's special tent they would have to come up with the readies. The metals, the woods, the materials were already in their homes, packed on their donkeys and tucked away for a rainy day. As realisation dawned, Moses announced an offering to end all offerings.

Gold, silver, bronze; wool dyed red, blue or purple; linen and goat hair; acacia wood and leather; olive oil and gemstones. If the people had it and were willing to give it, it would be used. It didn't end there. Moses wanted the skilled workers of the Israelites to give their time and energy to making this tent and all its furnishings. This was to be a group project. God had done the design. Now it was up to the people to do the rest. And so the collection began.

Nothing like it had been seen before or since. From dawn until dusk, people lined up to give however much or however little they wanted. From the youngest to the oldest, everybody found something they could bring. They gave up their jewellery, their spices, their clothes and their wood. They had been given the chance of a new start with God and they were not going to muck it up again.

'I DIDN'T MEAN TO GIVE ALL THAT WOOL!'

78

While the crowds poured in with their gifts, Moses appointed two people to oversee the work. They were skilled craftsmen, they were workers of imagination and planning, and they were remarkably cheap. Bezalel and Oholiab (not to be confused with Bezaloliab and Ohell who were two entirely different people) got the job and set to work. And still the money and the gifts poured in. It was like all the Blue Peter appeals, Red Nose Days, Children in Needs and Telethons rolled into one. It wasn't long before something happened that has never happened in the history of charity collections before or since. One of the people counting up all the gifts rushed to find Moses and said, 'Tell them to stop. We've got more than we need – we can't take anymore.'

So it was that God's special tent[7] was made. When every last

---

[7] People who like using long words called it a 'tabernacle' but 'special tent' will do.

stitch was stitched, curtain hook hooked, and oil lamp oiled, the people gathered for the opening ceremony. The tablets of stone with God's Ten Rules carved into them were placed in a special box, the lamps were lit and the incense was smoking away. The special bread arrived, which God had commanded should never be missing. Aaron and his children, who were to perform the first services, put on their magnificent gowns and robes. Everything was done just as God had said. Everything was ready. Now the people waited for one more thing, without which all their work would have been in vain.

Suddenly the skies went dark and a huge cloud covered the tent. The people stared, but all their fine work and craftsmanship had vanished. But as they peered through the dense, grey cloud, it was as though a small light had been switched on and was getting brighter and brighter. Soon the cloud could not be seen at all, and all the fabrics and objects that made up the tent could be seen clearly. The light got brighter and brighter until people could no longer bear to look at it. Before too long, even if anybody had dared to peep, they would have only seen bright, glorious light. A light seen nowhere on earth. A light that said to the people of Israel that, once again, God had kept his promise and had come to live among them.

Well, it had all been very exciting, and some of the children really should have gone to bed much earlier, but God coming to live with you isn't something you get to see every day. However, even the biggest and best of parties have to come to an end sometime, and with the cold light of dawn came the realisation that there was still a desert to cross and a home land to find.

The journey through the desert had taken on a familiar pattern. Every morning the people would collect the manna for their breakfast. Then the sacred tent would be taken down and rolled up to be carried with them to their next resting place, where it would be set up again, and God's cloud would cover it until darkness fell. Then the cloud turned into fire which gave enough light for the people to go and collect quails, which never failed to fall out of the sky for supper.

'PICNIC! WELL I DIDN'T EXPECT THIS MUCH QUAIL!'

After the escape from Egypt, the struggle through the Red Sea, and that terrible mistake at Sinai when it looked as though they had blown the chance of having God with them forever, life settled into a smooth routine. People were learning to live according to God's rules. It wasn't always easy, and being God's own people wasn't the picnic that some had thought. It was hard to do what was right all the time.

Meanwhile, Aaron and his family and other members of the house of Levi were learning how to act as priests for the people – making sure that the special tent was always set up right, that there was always enough oil for the lamps and that they didn't

EXODUS 29

burn too much incense (if they did, the smell could get right up their noses). However, just occasionally, there were little reminders that God really did mean what he said, and people should not become too laid back about keeping his rules. Take, for example, the time when two of Aaron's sons played around with a fire pan, and got more than their fingers burned. It had been a long day for Nadab and Abihu, but before they went off duty they had to get some incense to burn to the Lord. The altar for the incense was one of Bezalel the carpenter's finest pieces – carved from acacia wood and covered with gold, with each corner curving away like the horns of a bull. It spoke of God's majesty, a truly fitting symbol for the house of God. It stood dazzling within the sacred tent, but this day the two sons couldn't be bothered with their work. The sooner they got this last job done, the sooner they could go home. Little did they know that they were never going to go home again.

Whose idea it was to burn the incense in a firepan rather than on the altar we will never know, but hey, it was a bad idea. No sooner

LEVITICUS 10:1-9; 19

'I THINK WE NEED TO READ THE INSTRUCTIONS ONCE MORE'

'WHOA! TOO MUCH!'

'AARON WILL BE "INCENSED"!'

had the incense begun to burn than flames leapt all around the pan, and up and over Nadab and Abihu. It was the noise of the firepan falling from their charred and lifeless fingers that brought the others running. There in the middle of the tent were two bodies, where no bodies ought to be.

Moses could see what had happened, and looking at his brother Aaron and then at his barbecued nephews, he said quietly, 'You see. God must be respected. He has given his rules, all of his rules, for a purpose. It's not a game. It's literally a matter of life and death.'

The bodies were taken away, and Aaron continued with his priestly duties in a kind of daze. It was a hard way to learn a hard lesson, but Aaron could see the sense. He resolved to obey God, but there was one thing he couldn't do that day. Part of the sacrifice was meant to be eaten by the priests but, somehow, eating in the place where his sons had died was not something Aaron could face at the moment. Surely, just this once God would understand.

However, he did manage to pray the evening prayer. A prayer for protection for the people of Israel. A prayer of blessing that God had promised to answer if Aaron and his family prayed. Tonight, more than any other night, Aaron was conscious of the importance of this prayer being answered. Without the blessing and protection of God, he thought, we will all end up as burned bodies. So it was with a heavy heart, but also a sense of understanding, that the people's hope rested with God alone, that Aaron came outside the tent. As the people gathered in the light of the setting sun he raised his arm and proclaimed:

> Blessing and Protection,
> Mercy and Kindness,
> Goodness and Peace,
> Be yours from the Lord.
> Now and for ever.

LEVITICUS 13:1-6

IF YOUR SPOTS DO NOT TURN YOUR HAIR WHITE,
FOR A WEEK YOU'LL BE BANNED – AS IS RIGHT.
IF BY THEN THEY'VE NOT SPREAD,
PRIESTS CAN SEE YOU'RE NOT DEAD,
AND THEY'LL SAY, 'YOU CAN COME HOME TONIGHT'.

9 Census And Sensibility

NUMBERS 2

Even with all Moses' arrangements for letting others share the work, there were still a lot of people to get through this desert. 'There are an awful lot of people to get through this desert,' said Moses to God one day, during one of their regular chats. 'How many?' asked God. 'Loads,' said Moses. 'How many's that?' asked God. Moses thought for a while, and thought some more and said, 'Well, I don't know but it's a very big number.'

'Count them,' said God. 'Bloomin' heck!' said Moses, but not wanting to argue, set off to work out how he was going to manage this latest task.

'I TOLD AARON NOT TO COUNT SHEEP!'

It took a long time. Counting everybody's legs and dividing by two, as Aaron suggested, was an idea swiftly rejected. More popular was the idea of just counting the men. At least this would reduce the task a bit. Moses did have help from Aaron and a dozen

'I'VE RUN OUT OF FINGERS, CAN I BORROW YOURS?'

other men, but it still took all day, what with making sure totals matched, that people hadn't been counted twice, and with the several occasions when they lost their place in the crowd and had to start again. At last, all the figures were in and double-checked, and the grand total (men only) was announced:

603,550.

This was quite a number, and as they were walking further into the land and nearer and nearer to enemy tribes, it was of some comfort to know that there was such a huge army of men to call on. That was even after taking out the Levites, who would be excused fighting duty because they had to do their jobs in the sacred tent. Nowadays, if the answer to the question 'What did you do in the war daddy?' was 'Well I hung around the temple doing odd jobs. You know the kind of thing - trimming the oil lamps, polishing the woodwork and polishing off a couple of dozen sacrificial bulls a day,' Junior wouldn't be that impressed (nor would the bulls, come to think of it). However, for the people of Israel, it was important to honour the God who was with them and had promised to protect them, so it was no shame to be on duty in the chapel while the fighting was going on. Mind you, there were a lot of them at it. Of that big number that Moses had worked out, over 45,000 of them were Levites - so not much chance of getting out of putting money in the offering with all that number milling around with collecting bowls.

Apart from the priests, all the other men were expected to be ready to defend their people at a moment's notice. Of course, with that many people, giving a moment's notice was not going to be easy - you couldn't e-mail everyone, and if you tried sending a message round in groups you'd end up with your own

version of Israelite-Chinese Whispers. 'Move further forward, we're on the attack' would end up as 'Shove father over, he's lying on his back', which would give countless children a wonderful opportunity, but was absolutely no use at all for winning battles. This was where the silver trumpets came in. Two trumpets blowing was the sign to pack up, gather at the sacred tent and be ready to move on. One trumpet meant that Moses wanted a word with the tribe leaders. Three trumpets playing a medley of Egyptian Dance Tunes meant 'OK kids, very funny, but stop messing about'.

'LOOK AT THAT GIRL IN THE BANGLES'

'SHE'S WALKING LIKE AN EGYPTIAN!'

With these arrangements made, God moved away from the sacred tent, the two trumpets were blown and when the people had gathered Moses was able to say something many of us only dream about.
'Right gang,' he yelled, 'follow that cloud!'
So Sinai was left behind. You'd have thought the idea that at last they were moving on to the land God had promised would have given the people a sense of excitement and adventure. But no.

'MY FEET HURT'

'OWWW! SUNBURN'

'I NEED A WEE!'

'I'M THIRSTY'

'Our feet hurt. We're thirsty. We've got sunburn, and the people in the next tent kept us awake all last night. It's too far. How do we know we're not lost?

Why do kids think it's funny to shout "are we there yet" every ten steps?'

God was angry, the cloud bubbled with fury and suddenly the people who were complaining the loudest knew what it would have been like to have stayed in Egypt - because they were dead. Struck down by fire pouring out of the skies. That shut up those who were about to grumble... for a while.

Of course, it soon continued. Usually around mealtimes, as the kitchens were serving up manna pancakes - again. Nobody made jokes any more about 'Where's the maple syrup?' or 'Just a squeeze of lemon with mine' because it wasn't funny. Instead, some bright spark would simply murmur 'A few fried leeks and onions would go well with this' and then they were off - thinking back to the food there had been in Egypt. Forgotten were the nights when they had sat bent double in their huts, writhing in agony from bad backs and pulled muscles. The scars from the whips that had ripped into their flesh were still there, but they didn't seem to notice them anymore. The children still had nightmares about slave-drivers rampaging through their play-areas, scattering their games and bullying any child who dared to show fear or, even worse, began crying. But never mind all that, suddenly it all seemed to be worth it for a few cucumbers and a bit of roasted garlic. Maybe the heat of the desert was stopping them thinking properly, maybe they were just tired. Whatever the reason Moses had had enough, and he let God know about it.

'It's too big a job for me. I thought I was going to lead people to a chosen land, not sit around listening to them moaning about the menu. They want more meat, but where am I supposed to get meat from? I'm just a punchbag for everyone to have a go and it's not fair. In fact, I might as well be dead - at least I'd get some peace then.'

Given that God had just shown how easily he could destroy whingers, this was the moment when Moses might have thought he had gone just a bit too far. However, at least he had had the honesty to complain directly to God, instead of moaning to his family and friends like the rest of the Israelites did.

How many times would God have to demonstrate his love and his power? It was all very well Moses going on about how *he* couldn't provide the meat, but he hadn't provided *any* so far. Well, if they wanted meat they could have meat.

That evening a wind began to blow and, as the people had come to expect, the quails began to fall on the ground. And fall and fall and keep on falling. Soon there was quail as far as the eye could see. And further. Those who had not been satisfied with what God had been providing faithfully, day after day, could hardly believe their eyes. Their heads began to fill with pictures of roast quail, braised quail, quail pie, quail jam, quail surprise (just manna without any quail – that was the surprise), quail on toast, seared quail with a special desert dessert (that's a sort of quail mousse). But, before they could even put the camp fire on to a low flame, God highlighted the ail in quail and all those who had badgered for more meat fell ill. The realisation slowly dawned on them that they had been greedy and showed an incredible lack of trust in a God who had not let them down – ever. This realisation usually came just before they died... and they all did.

This left an awful lot of rotting quail lying around. Moses could see they had a choice – clear up or clear off. So they did the sensible thing. They went to Hazeroth.

IF THERE'S A GREEN PATCH ON YOUR WALL,
YOU SHOULD ASK THAT YOUR PRIEST PAYS A CALL.
'IT IS MILDEW, I'M SURE
AND IT'S BEEN HERE BEFORE.
IT'S TIME TO DEMOLISH IT ALL.'

LEVITICUS 14:35–45

10 ON THE BRINK

NUMBERS 13:1 – 14:45
DEUTERONOMY 1:19-33

Canaan. The people of Israel had talked about it, imagined it, dreamed about it and now they were nearly there. The land which God would give them was called Canaan, and it was just past the next desert and over the hill. You or I would have rushed off to be first over the border and pick out the best camping site. The people of Israel were more cautious. This may have had something to do with the fact that the land already had people living there. Somehow they didn't think the locals would take too kindly to a group of dusty, weather-beaten slaves turning up and playing a sort-of national version of 'I'm the King of the Castle'.

'DAD ARE WE NEARLY THERE YET?'

'OH YES!'

Before there was any racing for the borders, or people getting too carried away with dreams of their new home, God suggested they send a group in to spy out the land. Just a small crowd – twelve in fact. Large enough to help each other out if there was trouble, but small enough to be mistaken for a stray tourist group looking for their train (their camel-train, obviously). The twelve spies were sent on their way and the people waited for their return. Five days went by, then another five. After fifteen days, there were those who said, 'They're obviously having such a great time they can't drag themselves away.' After twenty days, there were those who thought not being able to drag themselves away might have more to do with being captured. After twenty-five days, one or two began to look round the desert and think, 'Well it's not too bad here.' When thirty days had gone by, and there was still no sign of them, their families were beginning to think of memorial services. By day thirty-five there were those who felt it was hopeless. But amongst all these people there were those who were still sure it would all work out, and kept their eyes on the horizon and not on the calendar.

36, 37, 38, 39... and then... On day 40, someone came running into the camp saying there was a cloud of dust in the distance, and dust usually meant somebody or something coming their way. Sure enough, as the day wore on, the cloud drew nearer and the people could make out shapes moving in their direction. The shapes looked big and round and – to be honest – rather purple. Casting their minds quickly over the twelve men who had been sent out, nobody could remember anyone who answered that description. But, try as they might, they couldn't make the biggest shape look like anything other than a giant bunch of grapes. Which it was. A bunch so enormous it took two men to carry it.

A crowd soon gathered round the twelve men, eager to hear about this new land where grapes grew as big as very big grapes. 'It's beautiful'; 'It's huge'; 'There's food everywhere'; 'We'll want for nothing'; 'It's splendid'; 'It's incredible'; 'It's just over there.' The twelve men were falling over themselves to add to the

'IT'S HUGE!'

'IT'S INCREDIBLE!'

'IT'S BEAUTIFUL!'

'WE'LL WANT FOR NOTHING!'

'IT'S SPLENDID!'

'THERE'S FOOD EVERYWHERE!'

'BUT...'

description, some, as you will have noticed, more successfully than others.

The crowd began muttering to themselves, talking over all that they had heard. Then one of the twelve said, quietly, 'But...'

It was only a small word but it shot through the assembled people like a bullet. Everyone paused and waited. In the history of the universe, much of the best news has had a 'But...' tagged on to the end.

We can build schools with fantastic science labs, brilliant sports halls and kitchens serving the best grub in town, but someone will insist on paying teachers to work there.

We can create digital, satellite and other funky kinds of television with eighty-five channels, but somebody will still say on a Friday night, 'There's nothing to watch.'

We can pluck up the courage to ask the nicest girl in the class out to the disco, but somebody will have already taught her the word 'No!'

The 'but' was to do with the people living there. Strong people, enormous people, lots of people. People whose very size and strength made you feel like grasshoppers, and would squash you before you even had a chance to rub your back legs together.

Of the twelve, only Caleb and Joshua stayed calm. 'We can defeat them,' Caleb said. He didn't add, 'If God is on our side, why are we afraid?' but I wouldn't be too far wrong if that was what he was thinking. However, it didn't really matter what he said or thought, as nobody was listening. They were too busy watching their dreams break and shatter all around them.

That night, wherever Moses went he could hear people crying. Children, women, grown men, all with one thought. It wasn't a new thought. Moses had heard it so many times before it was almost like a boring old friend. And, sure enough, as Moses wandered through the camp, it came out to greet him again and again.

'We'll be killed fighting for the land. It would have been better to die in Egypt, or even here in the desert.'

'BUT ISN'T GOD EVEN BIGGER?' The only ones who remained convinced that God would, as always, keep his word, were Moses, Aaron and two of the twelve who had gone to spy out the land – Caleb and Joshua. They were also pretty sure that he was not going to be happy with this champion whinge that was going on all around them. They were not wrong.

God, they should have known by now, answered prayer, and if the people's prayer was that they wished they could have died in the desert, they could have their answer. God declared that nobody over twenty would go into the land. Just as they had asked, they would die in the desert. Even

DEUTERONOMY 22:4

IT IS EASY TO FALL ON THE WAY,
IF YOUR DONKEY'S TOO LOADED WITH HAY.
IF WHILE TRAVELLING THE LAND,
YOU SEE ONE STRUGGLING TO STAND,
GO AND HELP HIM – YOU COULD MAKE HIS DAY.

the young ones would not be so young when they eventually arrived at their new land. It could have been theirs for the taking in a matter of days, but now God resolved that he would let the

Israelites continue wandering in the desert until they had learned to trust him. And God was prepared to let this continue, however long it took – even if it took forty years (and it did!).

Of the older generation, only Caleb and Joshua were told that they would still be around to enter Canaan after all that time.

When some of the people heard this, they refused to listen. 'This is ridiculous! Canaan is only a couple of sand-dunes

> COME ON! WE CAN DO THIS ALONE!

> OOPS!

away! Why not just march in and fight for the right to stay?' Well, it was a brave crowd that set off and, to be fair, they did all get to stay in the land... only they weren't alive. The Amalekites and the Canaanites, who already lived there, saw to that fairly decisively.

Even this didn't stop the grumbling and moaning. The people felt that they had been tricked. Moses had conned them into following him, and many of them were completely fed up. If God and Moses were not going to come up with the goods in terms of 'good plot of land with space for desirable residences', then they weren't going to listen to Moses any more. Moses was tempted to say that they hadn't listened to him very much in the first place, but he let it pass. Korah was the chief culprit, persuading all the Israelites that Moses had had his day, and that it was time for a new generation of leaders. Strong leaders, visionary leaders, leaders who wouldn't muck around with any of this 'forty-years-in-the-desert-until-we're-ready' nonsense. In fact, leaders like him and his mates Dathan and Abiram.

Moses was completely unfazed. If God had got him this far, he wasn't going to give up on him now. So, as calmly as possible, he talked to the crowds about how God had chosen him. If they wanted proof, he could give them proof. Moses asked the people what they would make of his leadership if Korah and his cronies and their families were to disappear into a hole in the ground and be buried alive. The cynics in the crowd hardly had time to think about it, when there was a rumble and cracking, a few assorted screams, and suddenly, there in the crowd was a gap previously occupied by Korah, his cronies and their families. The people of Israel couldn't believe their eyes.

Despite this, the people *still* weren't happy and were *still* plotting to challenge the leadership of Moses and Aaron. Incredibly, the more they rebelled, the more Moses and Aaron prayed for them. They knew what God could do but, despite everything, they loved these people. Yes, they were quarrelsome, selfish, faithless, and a whole load of other things, but these were the people God had allowed Moses to set free and, hey, a guy could get kind of attached when they'd been through some of the things they had been through.

It wasn't just Korah and his gang who ended up in a bit of a hole. All those who were complaining and arguing with Moses and Aaron found that they didn't feel so well. In fact many had to go and have a lie down. And many that lay down never got up again – ever. In the midst of all this, with people dropping like flies (well, like dead flies anyway), Moses and Aaron kept on praying, believing that God had called them to lead these people. After a while, God promised, one more time, to prove that Moses and Aaron had his blessing and were the guys he wanted to lead the nation. As soon as word of this got out, the people nervously started to look for cracks in the ground – they had been caught that way before.

This time, however, God was not proposing anything so drastic. Moses collected up twelve sticks, including the stick Aaron used, and promised that the stick which grew leaves belonged to his chosen leader. Now, if you've been keeping up with the journey of this special people, you might have expected something different. After all, when sticks have been involved previously, there has been blood, snakes, water pouring out of rocks and seas dividing into two. It wasn't that God had run out of ideas (as we shall see shortly – brace yourself for the story of Honest Balaam and his

'IT'S DONE NOTHING YET! COME ON SON! JUST FOR ME... ERM... US! NOT THE SNAKE THING, WE NEED LEAVES NOW... JUST A BUD WILL DO... COME ON...!!'

Discoursing Donkey – but I'm getting ahead of myself). No, God had always had a single idea. The rescue from Egypt, the crossing of the sea and the giving of the commands and laws were just part of the whole picture. What he wanted were people who belonged to him and would follow no other way but his. It wasn't a matter of turning over a new leaf but of being recreated – allowing God to get rid of their stubbornness and rottenness, making new lives that belonged to him. Which brings us back to the sticks sprouting leaves. Are you with me? Do try to keep up, you never know when there is going to be a test.

Well, it will come as no surprise to learn that when they looked, it was Aaron's stick that was growing leaves and almonds. After all, it was Aaron's family that God had already called to be the priests of his sacred tent. Grumbling was out. Listening and obeying was in. Well, at least Moses hoped so.

'AT LAST! YIPEE!'

Just to be sure people didn't forget, Aaron's stick was left in the special tent as a visual reminder of all that God was trying to say (and incidentally the almonds provided a handy snack for anyone feeling peckish in-between sacrifices).

It was shortly after this that Aaron died. Although the people were sad to see one of their great leaders pass away, and Moses lost not just his right-hand man but his brother, the people knew that God was working things out. They went on believing this, even when the people of Canaan attacked and took some of the Israelites hostage. God hadn't let them down so far, and Moses and the people didn't believe he was about to start now. Sure enough, when they attacked, victory was theirs, and the people promised God they would dedicate the land, and their lives, to him.

103

But, as ever, and despite all the warnings and evidence of God's faithfulness, it wasn't long before a bit of thirst on a day when the sun was extra-hot brought back the old problem. It seemed there was nothing the Israelites enjoyed more than a bloomin' good moan.

NUMBERS 21

WHY ARE WE STILL IN THIS DESERT?

I'VE GOT SAND IN PLACES I DIDN'T EVEN KNOW I HAD PLACES!

NO WATER AGAIN, WHAT DOES MOSES THINK HE'S UP TO?

I'M ABSOLUTELY FED UP AND NOW THERE'S ALL THESE SNAKES!

> I WONDER IF THEY'RE POISONOUS...

> YUP!

Around the camp, the voices trailed off one by one as the snakes, which had appeared from nowhere and were now everywhere, answered the question about whether or not they were poisonous, with one little bite.

It is amazing how imminent death from a snake bite can bring you to your senses. Soon a little delegation arrived at Moses' tent. The group apologised to Moses and, to be fair, they were a sorry-looking bunch – faces looking pale, serious expressions and eyes cast down to the ground (mind you, that was probably so they could keep a look out for the snakes). They wanted Moses to do something, so Moses talked to God who, as always, had the answer.

Moses was to make a snake out of bronze and put it on a pole. Not to make fun of the people who were *dying* but to give them a chance to show they were really sorry. It was quite simple really – all they had to do was to look at the snake on the pole and all would be well. Of course, God hoped that in looking up to the snake, they would remember to look up to him also. Sure enough, anyone who looked at the snake lived, even after they'd been bitten. Once again, God had shown to this group of faithless, complaining people that he was not going to leave them – all he asked for in return was their trust.

'THAT WILL TEACH YOU. I TOLD YOU TO CHEW YOUR FOOD!'

Of course, there were some stubborn so-and-so's who were sure they could sort out their own lives, and weren't going to do something like this. They were the ones that were being buried the following morning.

DEUTERONOMY 22:5

NO LASS SHOULD TRY BEING A LAD,
AND VICE VERSA IS EQUALLY BAD.
THE LORD WHO CREATED
HAS QUITE CLEARLY STATED
THAT ACTING LIKE THIS MAKES HIM SAD.

11 WONKY DONKEY

NUMBERS 22-25

The Canaanite army had been defeated, the Amorites were well and truly dealt with. The Israelites were on a roll (or a bagel or something... things were going pretty well anyway). However, the Israelites' neighbours were starting to get a bit nervous about this strange group of people who were wandering round the desert. Deep in the heart of Moab, something nasty was stirring – his name was King Balak.

KING BALAK OF MOAB

King Balak of Moab wanted shot of the Israelites (or knifed, drowned, garrotted... he wasn't fussy). He didn't want his people to end up like the Canaanites, in a life-termination scenario. Clearly, the thing to do was to get God on your side. And to do that you had to get somebody who was well in with God on your team. Balak knew just the bloke.

Down by the riverside in Pethor, was a prophet who seemed well-in with God. He was called Balaam, which made him sound like a baby sheep, although as Balak was to find out he was no pussy-cat. But enough of these mixed-metaphors. The point is King Balak wanted him to come and curse the Israelites, so that defeating them would be easy. What's more, he was prepared to pay. Well Balaam, wasn't sure, but he promised to talk to God about it and give King Balak his answer in the morning.

BALAAM

107

That night, God made it very clear that Balaam was to have nothing to do with this deal, pointing out that these people were his (God's) people and they needed blessing, not cursing. So that was Balaam's answer.

King Balak had heard people say that loving money was the root of all kinds of evil, but to his mind it was the route to any evil he wanted to carry out. He didn't take no for an answer, and came to Balaam offering more cash. Balaam was firm. He was not a man to be swayed by the offer of gold and silver beyond his wildest dreams.

Mind you, just think how much happiness he could create with all that money, and of course he would give most of it away to good causes. NO! NO! NO! Balaam gave himself a really good shaking. God had to be obeyed, but if it made King Balak happy, he would ask God once again what it was he wanted him to do. God, who thought the whole matter had been cleared up long before, said Balaam could go with King Balak if he really wanted. 'Just make sure you still obey me,' called God after Balaam. But Balaam didn't hear, so eager was he to rush after King Balak and get his hands on the money.

A larger tent, with better furnishings; perhaps a whole string of junior prophets working under him in his own little business (Futurewise plc), all these things were going through Balaam's head as he rode on his donkey with the Moabites. His thoughts were interrupted as the donkey swerved off the road. It took Balaam a good while, and the use of a heavy stick, before he could get the donkey back on the road and continue his journey.

'Stupid animal,' he was thinking, and wondering if he could trade it in for a new model on his return, when he let out a huge yell, and used the kind of language that I'm not allowed to write down here. The donkey had swerved again, dragging Balaam's foot along the adjoining wall. It was time to use that big stick again.

The journey carried on, with Balaam concentrating on the donkey, and wondering what the stubborn animal was going to do next. What he was going to do next was sit down in the middle of the road and, stick or no stick, he was not going to move.

Balaam raised his stick to thrash the donkey again when a voice said, 'Stop it!' Balaam looked around. There was nobody in sight, apart from the Moabites, and they were nearly out of sight as they carried on their journey regardless. 'Why do you keep on beating me?' asked the voice. Balaam looked down – it was the donkey talking! Balaam scowled at him; 'You made me look stupid,' he said, pausing only briefly to think, 'I

109

am standing in the middle of the road talking to a donkey... how stupid do I want to look?' The donkey continued, 'Have I ever let you down before?' Now this was a good point, although Balaam did think that the donkey had never spoken to him before, so perhaps previous actions didn't count. 'Did it not occur to you that there was a reason? Well there was, look.'

Balaam turned around, not knowing what he was going to see. He didn't expect to see the (big) angel that was standing there with a (big) sword (few people ever do). A few moments before, Balaam had been thinking that if he'd had a sword, he could have put an end to the donkey once and for all. He just hoped the angel didn't have similar plans for him.

Now the angel spoke. Donkeys? Angels? Where would it all end? The angel wanted to make sure that Balaam heard the end of the message he had missed by rushing off the day before. The point was that God would have preferred Balaam to stay where he was, but if he *insisted* on going, it must be to speak God's messages and not for any *money* King Balak could give him.

Balaam's dreams of untold wealth and a Hebrew pop star lifestyle faded away, but the angel didn't – and, more importantly, neither did the sword. So Balaam agreed to do what God wanted and went on his way, on the donkey. Who never, ever, said another word.

King Balak welcomed Balaam, and began talking about money straightaway. Balaam was firm – 'I will only tell you what God wants me to say, and not what you want to hear,' was his opening line. King Balak wasn't really listening, but took him off to a point which overlooked the Israelite camps. Balaam prepared his sacrifice to offer to the Lord, and King Balak settled down to hear the curse, which he was sure spelled doom for the Israelites.

(Foolish man – everybody knows that d – o – o – m spells doom.)

When Balaam came with the message, King Balak sat up, eager to hear what nasty end God had in store for the Israelites.

Balaam's message went something like this:

**KING BALAK WANTS TO HEAR THE WORST,
TO HEAR ME RANT AND RAVE AND CURSE,
BUT GOD SAYS 'NO, THESE PEOPLE ARE MINE,
SO LEAVE THEM ALONE, THEY'RE DOING FINE.**

His message delivered, Balaam was saddling up his donkey and getting ready to go home, when King Balak had another idea. This was a big nation and cursing them all was perhaps too much to ask. Perhaps Balaam could just focus on a small part of the Israelites. Maybe pick one or two tribes and start with them? Balaam wasn't very hopeful, but if the King wanted him to try again he would. Shortly afterwards he came back with another message...

> GOD DOES NOT FIB, HE DOES NOT LIE.
> THOSE PEOPLE ARE SAFE AND I'LL TELL YOU WHY:
> IT'S NOT THAT GOD IS ACTING ON A WHIM -
> HE SAVED THESE PEOPLE AND THEY'RE SPECIAL TO HIM.
> HE LIVES AMONG THEM IN HIS OWN SPECIAL TENT.
> THAT'S ALL YOU'RE GOING TO GET SO IT'S TIME I WENT.

DEUTERONOMY 22:6

> A NEST ON THE GROUND, GOODNESS ME!
> YOU COULD TAKE THE BIRDS HOME FOR YOUR TEA.
> BUT DON'T TAKE THE MOTHER,
> LEAVE HER THERE FOR ANOTHER
> OR ALLOW HER TO FLY AWAY, FREE.

This was not the answer King Balak wanted. Again. Perhaps they were in the wrong place. Perhaps the prophet's 'magic' wasn't going to work here. So he moved Balaam somewhere else, and asked him to have another go. This was all getting a bit tedious, and to make matters worse, Balaam wasn't even going to get paid. Balaam soon dismissed this temptation when he thought about the big angel and his big sword. He couldn't be certain, but he was sure the donkey kept giving him a funny look as well, or maybe he was just permanently cross-eyed. So, knowing things weren't going to change, Balaam went back to the sacrificing, and waited to hear what God was going to say this time.

King Balak was ready for him. 'Look, forget the singing, chanting stuff – just give me the message.' But Balaam was a prophet and he had his reputation to look after. When it came to pious prophetic pronouncements, people had certain expectations – they wanted a bit of a show, and King Balak was going to get the song whether he liked it or not.

> ISRAEL IS LOVED BY GOD AND THAT WILL LAST FOR EVER.
> IF YOU WANT TO KNOW WHEN THEY'LL BE CURSED, THE ANSWER IS 'NEVER'.
> HE'S GOT PLANS TO MAKE THEM POWERFUL EXAMPLES TO US ALL
> AND IF YOU TRY AND BEAT THEM, YOU'RE THE ONE WHO'LL FALL.
> CURSING THEM IS REALLY A BAD THING TO DO.
> YOU COULD SOON FIND THAT THE CURSE COMES BOUNCING BACK TO YOU.

King Balak was fed up. What a total waste of time this had all been. One thing was certain, Balaam was not getting any of his money. Well, as we know, disappointing though this may have been, this was no surprise to Balaam.

Balaam packed up, reloaded his donkey and set off for home, but not before giving one last message.

'O King, I've one more thing to say, I tell you this is true -

God's enemies will be destroyed and that means poor old you!'

'YOU!'

HONEST JOSEPH

DEUTER-
ONOMY 22:8

IF YOUR BUILDER IS NOT ALL THAT WISE,
AND A FLAT ROOF IS WHAT HE SUPPLIES,
ROUND THE ROOF BUILD A WALL.
THEN IF SOMEONE SHOULD FALL,
IT WON'T BE YOUR FAULT IF HE DIES.

'BEN, COME DOWN
'ERE 'AN 'ELP US
BRING THESE
BRICKS UP'

There is a PS to this story. It would be lovely to think that Balaam had learned from all his experiences to serve God completely, and not to rely on magic and other things which *should* play *no part* in the life of a genuine prophet of God. Sad to say, this was not to the case. Some time later, he persuaded some of the people of Israel to worship a false god, and many died as a result. It appears that his donkey was not there on that occasion to put him right, or history might have been very different.

'AND YOU THOUGHT I WAS A SILLY ASS!'

'BILLS, BILLS, BILLS... OH... AND THIS SLAVE WITH A FOREIGN STAMP ON HIM'

DEUTERO-NOMY 23:15

IF A SLAVE FROM A LAND FAR AWAY,
TURNS UP ON YOUR DOORSTEP ONE DAY,
LET HIM IN – THAT'S QUITE COOL.
THERE'S JUST ONE GOLDEN RULE –
YOU'RE STUCK WITH HIM NOW – LET HIM STAY.

YES, YOU CAN STAY BUT YOU'RE TAKING TOO MANY LIBERTIES. THAT'S *MY* RUBBER DUCK!

DEUTERONOMY 23:24

IF YOUR NEIGHBOUR SAYS
'COME SEE MY FRUIT',
HE REALLY WILL NOT GIVE A
HOOT,
IF WHILE YOU ARE THERE,
YOU EAT ALL THAT YOU DARE,
BUT DON'T TAKE IT AWAY OR
HE'LL SHOOT.

12 Moses: The Final Chapter

NUMBERS 27

Unaware of all that was going on in the hills around, Moses had other things to think about.

He wasn't getting any younger, and he knew that God had meant it when he said he would not be allowed to enter the Promised Land. That meant there had to be a someone to take over. The people needed a leader – but who?

Moses thought back to that time in the desert, when he had stood in front of a burning bush. What qualities of leadership did he have back then? He started to make a list. It wasn't a very long list. In fact, as lists go, it was non-existent. It was simply that God had chosen him. That was the answer! He knew that the new leader had to be *God's* choice. He could have looked around the people and singled out the trained warriors, the good organisers, the popular ones, the good-looking ones, the ones who would be foolish enough to volunteer for the job; but it had to be the person *God* wanted.

God told Moses his choice. The people would see who it was when Moses brought him before Eleazar the new high priest of the sacred tent.

117

When Aaron died, his son had taken over his responsibilities, and so it was to Eleazar that Moses brought the man God had chosen. The crowds were gathered, straining to see who it was. For those of a betting nature, Caleb was clearly one of the front runners. He had been chosen as one of the twelve to go into Canaan, and he had been the only one who tried to convince the people of Israel that, with God on their side, defeating the Canaanites would not be a problem.

> ISN'T THAT THE SON OF NUN?
>
> DON'T BE SILLY! HE MUST BE THE SON OF SOMEONE
>
> NOT NONE. *NUN!*
>
> SON OF A NUN? NO, THAT CAN'T BE RIGHT
>
> CAREFUL! THESE JOKES COULD BECOME A NASTY *HABIT!*

It wasn't Caleb walking alongside Moses, though. A whisper went round the crowd as they saw the chosen one. 'Isn't that the son of Nun?' asked one member of the crowd. 'Don't be silly,' muttered another, 'he must have been the son of somebody.' 'Not None, NUN!' said the first. 'The son of a nun? No, that can't be right. They're not allowed.' No doubt the argument could have gone on for hours, but their squabble was swallowed up in the roars of the people as they welcomed their new leader, Joshua. There was still a lot to do before Moses could fully hand over control. He had to ensure that the people understood that following God was not just a now-and-again thing. After all this time they should have known, but people are stubborn and often far too fond of doing things their way rather than God's. It wasn't simply a case of being in the right land with the right place of worship and God's laws written down on stone in the special box. All these things mattered, but what they had to understand was that to have God as their friend affected every moment of every day of their lives. There was no area where they could say, 'Well, I'll please myself here.' God was interested in the clothes they wore, the food they ate, the way they celebrated festivals, how they treated friends and strangers, how they harvested their crops. Because he cared so much, no detail was too small. Moses ensured that all these things were written down. You can still find the book today in the Bible. It's book number five in the first section of the Bible and it's called:

'WELL, THAT'S THE WORSHIP STUFF DONE! NOW WE CAN PARTY!'

DEUTERONOMY

If that's a bit of a mouthful, you could always call it 'Second Law' – 'cos that's what the word means. Not that these were new laws or variations on the original laws – they were the same – Moses just needed to remind people. As he spoke to them, he went over not just the rules, but their history. From slavery to freedom. From the cities of Egypt to the deserts of Sinai. From a people

> **DEUTERONOMY 24:5**
>
> ON THE HAPPIEST DAY OF HIS LIFE,
> A GROOM SHOULD BE FREE OF ALL STRIFE,
> IF WAR RAISES ITS HEAD,
> HE CAN JUST STAY IN BED,
> AND SEND IN A NOTE FROM HIS WIFE.

with no place to call their own to a people on the border of a new land. It was their story – the good bits (and there had been plenty), and the bad bits (and there had been too many). It hadn't all been groaning and complaints, although some days it felt like it. There had been times of singing and dancing (like when they made it across a seemingly uncrossable sea), and days of wonder and splendour (like when God thundered from the mountain top, or his cloud of glory came down to fill the sacred tent).

The trouble was not that people would forget, but that many of the people alive now, as Moses faced death, had been born after all those events. They didn't need *reminding* of their history. Many of them needed to hear it for the first time. A new generation had grown up and, when the time came to enter Canaan, only Joshua and Caleb would be able to talk of the days of escape from Egypt and say, 'We were there' (they had the T-shirt).

The young men, women and children knew where they were going and were eager to get there. Moses wanted to make sure they knew about where they had come, from and the price that others had paid for their freedom – there had been pain and death and suffering along the way. The cost would only be worth it if the Israelites became a people who were not ashamed to belong to God, and who told the world how much he deserved to be worshipped.

Moses told the stories so the people would tell their children. Their children would, in turn, tell their children and so it would go on down the years and across the centuries.

Thousands of years later, a young wandering preacher called Jesus was asked to name the most important law of all. He didn't hesitate. He simply repeated words first spoken by Moses and repeated across the generations. Words that Moses had used to sum up all that he wanted the people to know:

'Listen Israel.
The Lord God is the only true God.
Love him with every fibre of your being.
Your heart, soul and strength.
Love him, love him, love him.
And then love him some more.'

Of course, not only did the people need to hear the laws again, but they needed to be reassured that God's agreement with their ancestors counted for them too. There was no sell-by date to God's commitment. He would continue to lead and guide this new generation, and the one after that, and the one after that...
Nobody who claimed their right to belong to the Family of God would ever find that the guarantee had run out. But it was one thing to know that this was your right, and quite another to choose to use that right. It was all very well being *told* of the choices your ancestors had made, but what choice would the people make *now*? This was what Moses wanted to know.

Like the previous generations, these people had to decide for themselves. God had made it very plain what was expected. It wasn't as though anybody had to try and work out for themselves what God's rules were – it had even been written down. But knowing the rules and obeying them were two completely different matters. Moses had made his choice, and he was content to die knowing that the future lay in God's hands. Now it was the turn of every man, woman and child to make their own choice.

'What will it be?

GOD...   **...OR SELF?**

TRUTH...   **...OR LIES?**

LIFE...   **...OR DEATH?**

For an old man, Moses had a powerful voice and this last challenge rang out through the gathered people. What they answered from their hearts only they knew... and God. The time had come. The next journey for Moses would take him not into the Promised Land, but on a journey with God into death. He had one final walk to make on this earth before then. Up into the Abirim mountains, where he would be able to look out at the land of Canaan. Not to fill his heart with bitterness and sorrow because God had said he couldn't go, but to rejoice at the part he had been allowed to play in this amazing journey of a special people.

DEUTERONOMY 32-34

Before he set out, he had a final song to sing. He wanted these crazy, frustrating, stubborn, loyal, loveable people to hear once more about how much God loved them.

Moses sang out. A song of God's power and strength. A song that spoke of God as a rock – solid and dependable – living with people who seemed to find it hard to keep going his way.

It was the song of a people who had come from nowhere, and slowly but surely were being shaped into the people of God. There was failure and suffering, death and destruction in the words that Moses sang. And running through it all like a constant chorus was the truth that the Lord is God, and that he and no other has the right to our loyalty, our love and our lives.

The song echoed across the crowds. Its meaning was clear, and the people knew what they had to do. If God loved them and had done so much for them, surely he was worth obeying? It was so hard to do, but there weren't many listening that day who didn't know that it was up to them to live lives that proved to the whole world that they were not just any people – they were God's people.

As the song ended, Moses had some special words for the tribes of Israel:

LEVI – THE FAITHFUL PRIESTS WITH THE GREAT RESPONSIBILITY OF KEEPING THE PEOPLE ON TRACK WITH GOD

BENJAMIN – LOVED BY GOD

REUBEN – A SMALL TRIBE BUT ONE THAT WOULD TRIUMPH

JUDAH – A PEOPLE WHO GOD WOULD LISTEN TO

JOSEPH – A TRIBE WHO WOULD DRINK DEEPLY OF ALL THE BLESSINGS GOD PROVIDED

DAN – A NERVOUS, JUMPY PEOPLE. THEY MUST LEARN TO TRUST GOD

ISSACHAR – THEIR WEALTH WILL COME FROM THE LAND. THEY HAD TO SHARE THE BLESSINGS WITH OTHERS

ZEBULUN – THEY WILL SAIL OVER THE SEAS AND LET OTHER LANDS KNOW THAT GOD IS WITH THEM

GAD – THE LAND THEY HAVE WILL BECOME MORE. GOD WILL BLESS THEM

NAPTHALI – GOD IS PLEASED WITH THEM. HE WILL BLESS THEM, THEY MUSTN'T SQUANDER WHAT HE GIVES

ASHER – A TRIBE WHOSE BLESSINGS WILL PUT THE GLORIES OF THE OTHER TRIBES INTO THE SHADOW; BUT THERE WILL BE NO JEALOUSY OR BITTERNESS. THE REST OF THE NATION WILL COME TO LOVE THIS RICH AND POWERFUL PEOPLE

> **DEUTERONOMY 24:19**
>
> WHEN THE TIME COMES TO HARVEST YOUR CROPS,
> LEAVE THE REST OF THE CORN WHERE IT DROPS.
> LET THE POOR HAVE THEIR SHARE,
> REALLY SHOW THAT YOU CARE,
> IT WILL SAVE THEM A TRIP TO THE SHOPS.

And so, with these words ringing in their ears, Moses left the people and set off for the hills. They never saw him again but, as the people sat round the camp fires each evening and told their stories, often the children would ask again for the

WHO ARE THESE GUYS?

MALC'

Schools-worker, charity coordinator, youth pastor, local radio celebrity, church minister are just some of the 'work experience' that Malc' can fill in on a CV. He has also, at different times, had an ear pierced and dyed his hair green. He devours books, films and black coffee in between working for a church in Coventry, studying in Oxford and socialising with anyone who will talk to him. He has written for SU's *Quest* Bible notes and *SALT* material and now, of course, the blockbuster *Bible Bites* series.

IAN

Shropshire lad, Ian, was born and brought up on a small sheep farm. His childhood dislike of the outdoors, lack of computer games, the everlasting rain and his phobia of chickens (linked to a vicious attack by 300 manic hens when he was four) led him to the drawing board and he's been drawing ever since. Despite his early acquaintances being mainly of the four-legged variety, Ian has progressed through a variety of academic institutions and is now a trainee solicitor working in Sheffield, where he worships at St Thomas's Church.

story of the boy who found it hard to fit in with the Hebrews, the Egyptians or the Midianites. A man who, when he stopped to listen to a bush, discovered who he really was – a child of God with a job to do.

Moses had taken the people had far as he could. Now it was Joshua's turn to take on the task of keeping them on the right road. But that is another story for another time. Like Moses, we too have come to the end of this particular road. There will come a time to reveal what sort of a job Joshua did, and to tell you of some of the people who came to rule Israel after him.

Until then, in the words of Aaron:

Blessing and protection,
Mercy and kindness,
Goodness and peace,
Be yours from the Lord.
Now and forever. Amen.